Essential Contract Law for SQE1 provides a structured, concise yet comprehensive approach to key principles of contract law to support those embarking upon SQE preparation. The clarity of the concepts is commendable and the multiple choice questions provide useful practice opportunities.

Professor Lisa Webley, *Birmingham Law School, University of Birmingham, UK*

The outstanding level of clarity and focus along with its supportive features makes this the ideal SQE contract law text.

André Naidoo, *Senior Lecturer at De Montfort University, UK and author of* Complete Contract Law

A timely preparatory manual that provides a detailed overview of all relevant topics included in SQE1 Contract Law. Perfectly aligned with SRA assessment objectives, focusing on functional and practical aspects of practicing law in England and Wales.

Dr Pia Rebelo, *City University London, UK*

Essential Contract Law for SQE1

Essential Contract Law for SQE1 explains the key principles of contract law in a clear, concise, and easy-to-understand style. Written specifically for SQE study, this book covers all of the topics contained in the syllabus for the contract law subject area in SQE1 Functioning Legal Knowledge (FLK) assessments.

The book provides a clear and structured approach with opportunities to apply the relevant principles to contract law. It also includes a range of features designed to help you test and confirm your knowledge of contractual legal principles, including:

- Revision points: Each chapter concludes with a concise list of key revision points.
- Multiple choice questions: Each section of the book provides multiple choice questions following the SQE1 question format (with answers to enable you to test your knowledge).

Part of Routledge's Essential Law for SQE1 series, this concise and accessible text provides a clear understanding of the key contractual principles and the core rules that underpin contract law and will enable you to test your assessment skills. Without the assumption of any prior knowledge of contract law, it is suitable for both undergraduates and non-law graduates.

Fred Motson is a senior lecturer in law at the Open University, where he has taught since 2020.

Stephen Bunbury is a reader in law at the University of Westminster, where he has taught since 2006.

Essential Law for SQE1
Series editor: Wendy Laws

Essential Law for SQE1 is a series of concise textbooks aligned to the latest SQE1 curriculum. Providing candidates with an accessible summary of the core principles in each area of law, the style of each book is precise, with bullet-point lists summarizing key information and revision points concluding each chapter. The books also feature multiple choice questions with answers, example problem questions and a glossary of key cases.

Essential Tort Law for SQE1
Wendy Laws

Essential Dispute Resolution for SQE1
Ben Waters

Essential Business Law and Practice for SQE1
Bill Davies

Essential Land Law for SQE1
Mohammad Sabuj

Essential Legal System and Legal Services for SQE1
Ian Bowden and Zaman F. Kala

Essential Criminal Law and Criminal Practice for SQE1
James Thornton, Amanda Parker and Orla Slattery

Essential Constitutional and Administrative Law for SQE1
Zaman F. Kala and Ian Bowden

Essential Contract Law for SQE1
Fred Motson and Stephen Bunbury

For more information about this series, please visit: www.routledge.com/

Essential Contract Law for SQE1

Fred Motson and Stephen Bunbury

Routledge
Taylor & Francis Group
LONDON AND NEW YORK

Designed cover image: Denys Polhun/iStock/Getty Images Plus/Getty Images

First published 2025
by Routledge
4 Park Square, Milton Park, Abingdon, Oxon OX14 4RN

and by Routledge
605 Third Avenue, New York, NY 10158

Routledge is an imprint of the Taylor & Francis Group, an informa business

British Library Cataloguing-in-Publication Data
A catalogue record for this book is available from the British Library

Library of Congress Cataloging-in-Publication Data
Names: Motson, Frederick, author. | Bunbury, Stephen, author.
Title: Essential contract law for SQE1 / Fred Motson and Stephen Bunbury.
Other titles: Essential contract law for Solicitors Qualifying Examination 1
Description: Abingdon, Oxon [UK]; New York, NY: Routledge, 2025. |
Series: Routledge's essential law for sqe1 | Includes bibliographical references and index.
Identifiers: LCCN 2024046536 | ISBN 9781032642147 (hardback) | ISBN 9781032642109 (paperback) | ISBN 9781032642161 (ebook)
Subjects: LCSH: Contracts – England – Examinations, questions, etc. |
Contracts – Wales – Examinations, questions, etc. | Solicitors Qualifying Examination.
Classification: LCC KD1554 .M69 2025 | DDC 346.4202/2076–dc23/eng/20241008
LC record available at https://lccn.loc.gov/2024046536

ISBN: 978-1-032-64214-7 (hbk)
ISBN: 978-1-032-64210-9 (pbk)
ISBN: 978-1-032-64216-1 (ebk)

DOI: 10.4324/9781032642161

Typeset in The Sans
by Apex CoVantage, LLC

To our children: Augustus and Beatrice; Elise and Ethan. You have not made actually writing this any easier, but you make our lives better every day.

Contents

About the authors

Fred Motson is a senior lecturer in law at the Open University. Fred has led contract law modules at all levels from foundation stage to postgraduate study, across a number of UK universities. He has extensive experience in teaching contract law outside of the traditional full time face-to-face environment, specialising in teaching contract law (and other legal subjects) to students learning part-time, at a distance, or from countries outside the UK. Fred has for a number of years held senior examiner roles with multiple legal regulatory bodies, which has given him considerable insight into how legal professional qualifications are assessed. In writing this book, he has sought to reflect the clear, straightforward, and practical approach required for successful legal study in this context.

Stephen Bunbury is a reader in law at the University of Westminster, where he has taught and led contract law for nearly two decades at foundation, undergraduate, and postgraduate level and for those wishing to practise law. He has acted as an expert in contract law as a consultant editor for a leading contract law textbook and has contributed to a revision text in contract law. Although he has research expertise in disability law, equality law, and legal education, his scholarship expertise lies in contract law and consumer law. He particularly has a passion for ensuring contract law is accessible to students from all levels and adopts a practical approach to understanding contract law. This book reflects his passion for studying contract law, whether it be undergraduate, postgraduate, or for those studying for the SQE.

Table of Cases

United States of America

Table of Legislation

United Kingdom

Introduction

This book provides a clear, concise explanation of contract law. Its focus is on those areas which fall within the assessment specification for the *Solicitors Qualifying Examination Part 1 Functioning Legal Knowledge* ("SQE1").

The style of the book reflects the SQE1 assessment specification:

- The SQE1 assessment requires knowledge and understanding of fundamental legal principles and the ability to apply them.
- Candidates are not required to recall specific case names or statutory provisions (except where they are normally used in practice to describe a legal principle).
- Candidates will be tested on the current law and will not be tested on the historical development of the law.

In order to reflect these requirements, the book explains the current key principles of the law in a clear, easy to follow style. Principles are introduced and illustrated by reference to realistic factual examples. References to key cases and statutes are provided.

This approach enables the book to provide a fluent narrative account of key principles which is clear and accessible, making it easier for the reader to understand the principles, remember them, and apply them in an assessment.

Key features to assist learning

Revision Points: Each chapter concludes with a concise list of key revision points.

Multiple Choice Questions: The SQE1 assessment uses multiple choice questions to test understanding of key principles. Multiple choice questions, following the SQE format, are provided at the end of each section of the book (with answers at the end of the book).

DOI: 10.4324/9781032642161-1

PART 1

Formation of a contract

1 Offer and acceptance

1.1 Chapter overview

This chapter will focus on two fundamental principles of contract formation: offer and acceptance, often referred to as the agreement stage. It will distinguish between two types of contracts, namely bilateral and unilateral contracts. The chapter will go on to consider the difference between an offer and an invitation to treat. It will discuss the rules concerning the communication and termination of an offer. It will continue by focusing on the legal rules as to what amounts to a valid acceptance and the rules governing this area of law, which is often tricky and complex. It will conclude by putting this all together.

1.2 What is a contract?

A legally binding contract is an agreement between two or more parties that involves an exchange of promises with the intention that the agreement will be legally enforceable. It allows the innocent party to sue in breach of contract, which entitles the innocent party to the usual remedy of damages (a sum of money paid to the innocent party to compensate for the breach, discussed later in Chapter 16) in the event of breach. It involves an exchange of promises by two or more parties that can be regarded as a binding agreement in law. Contracts can be made orally and in writing as there are no legal formalities prescribed in determining the form of most contracts.[1]

1.2.1 Bilateral and unilateral contracts

Different rules and exceptions apply to different types of contracts. It is therefore important at this early stage to distinguish between the two types of contracts that exist in contract law.

Bilateral contract

A bilateral contract consists of both parties making promises. This always involves an exchange of promises. For example, I buy a coffee in the coffee shop for £3. I promise to pay £3. In return the coffee shop promises to provide me with a cup of coffee.

1 Although there are some exceptions, notably contracts for the creation or disposal of an interest in land, S53 Law of Property Act 1925.

DOI: 10.4324/9781032642161-3

Unilateral contract

In a unilateral contract, only one party makes a promise in relation to a specified act.[2] The other party is not promising to do anything. However, if the other party chooses to carry out the act, they simultaneously accept and perform the contract. For example, I offer to pay a reward of £500 for someone who finds my lost cat, Bunny (an act). I am the only one promising to pay the reward of £500; no one is obliged to go and look for my cat (the act). The reward will be payable on full completion of the act – if someone does look for, and find, Bunny.[3]

1.2.2 The requirement for agreement

For there to be a legally binding contract, the parties must have reached an agreement. This stipulates the existence of a legally enforceable agreement between the parties. The courts have developed an objective test in determining whether a legally binding contract exists by looking at a party's intention. The objective approach to finding agreement means that the court will ask whether a (hypothetical) "reasonable person" who saw what the parties said and did would conclude that they had reached agreement.[4] In order to find agreement, there must be a clear and valid offer by one party (the offeror) which has been met with acceptance from the other party (the offeree).

1.3 Offer

It is important to identify whether the person has by their words or conduct made a valid offer in law, which is intended to be legally binding if it is met with acceptance. If this is satisfied, there is a valid offer in law capable of being accepted. An offer can be made to specific people or to the entire world.[5] In some situations, it is difficult to decipher whether a valid offer exists. It is therefore important to distinguish between a valid offer and an "invitation to treat". Understanding this is crucial in terms of identifying whether there is a legally binding contract. Without a valid offer, there can be no contract. See Figure 1.1 for requirements for an offer.

1.3.1 Distinguishing between an offer and an invitation to treat

In determining whether a valid agreement has been reached, it is important to understand whether a valid offer has been made. The courts will look at various factors to establish this and have developed general rules in different circumstances. An offer once accepted has contractual significance, while an invitation to

2 *Carlill v Carbolic Smoke Ball Co* [1893] 1 QB 256.
3 *Great Northern Railway Company v Witham* [1873] LR 9 CP 16; *Errington v Errington* [1952] 1 KB 290.
4 *Smith v Hughes* (1871) LR 6 QB 597.
5 See *Carlill v Carbolic Smoke Ball Co* [1893] 1 QB 256 as an example.

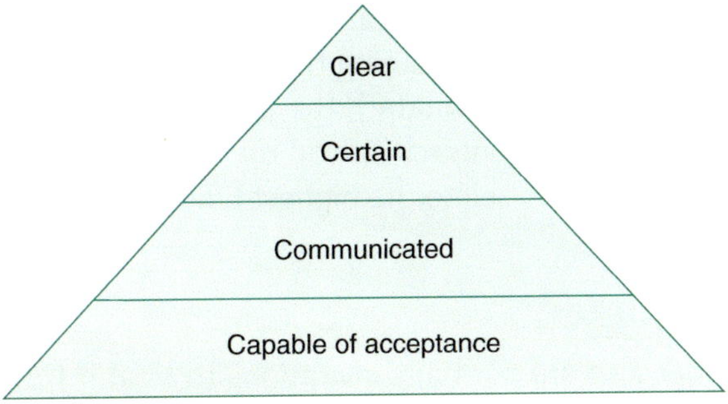

Figure 1.1 Requirements for an offer

treat is a preliminary stage in the negotiation process. It is an invitation to the other party to make an offer. Distinguishing between an offer and invitation is crucial in understanding whether a valid offer exists. Deciphering whether the language used is certain is an important factor in determining whether a valid offer exists.[6] There are certain situations which apply in various situations during the contract formation process.

Advertisements

In general, an advertisement is merely an invitation to treat, for example an advertisement on a website. There is no contractual significance, which makes sense otherwise the person or company advertising their goods or services would be bound to supply unlimited goods or services to everyone in the world who claims to accept the offer. However, there is an exception to the rule where the particular advertisement shows a clear intention to be bound by its terms, and in such a case the advertisement will be considered to be a unilateral offer to the world.[7]

Display of goods

A display of goods will amount to an invitation to treat.[8] For example, a display of goods on a supermarket shelf or clothes shop. The offer is not made until you reach the checkout and therefore there is no contractual significance until the contract is concluded at the checkout.

Auctions

An advertisement about an auction amounts to an invitation to treat. During the auction the auctioneer requests for bids amount to an invitation to treat, bidders

6 *Gibson v Manchester City Council* [1979] 1 All ER 972. Cf *Storer v Manchester City Council* [1974] 1 WLR 1403.

7 *Carlill v Carbolic Smoke Ball Co* [1893] 1 QB 256.

8 *Fisher v Bell* [1961] 1 QB 394 and *Pharmaceutical Society of Great Britain v Boots Cash Chemist Ltd* [1953] 1 QB 401.

make offers which the auctioneer is free to accept or reject.[9] However, where an auction is held "without reserve" (meaning the auctioneer must sell to the highest bidder as there is no minimum amount), the auctioneer is obliged to sell to the highest bidder as a unilateral contract ("if you make the highest bid, I will sell you the goods") exists. A refusal to sell to the highest bidder would result in a claim for breach of contract.

Invitations to tender

Invitations to tender also are normally invitations to treat.[10] However, there is an exception where a statement is made that the person inviting tenders promises to accept the highest tender. In these situations a unilateral contract will be formed with the person submitting the highest tender before the deadline.[11]

1.3.2 Communication of an offer

A fundamental principle is that an offer must be communicated.[12] Therefore, a party must have the requisite knowledge and must be aware of the offer. Communication of an offer can be in writing or orally. If an offer is not communicated, there cannot be a valid contract, as a party will not be bound if they are not aware of the offer. For example, Bob returns a lost dog by the name of Trigger to Shahid. When he returns the lost dog, he is not aware that Shahid has placed an advert in the park where Shahid offers to pay £100 to anyone who finds Trigger. As Bob is not aware of the offer, he will not be entitled to the reward of £100 even though he has found Trigger. Certain issues also arise where there are two identical offers known as "cross-offers". In cases such as these, neither party knows of the other offer at the time of communicating their own offer. Therefore, neither party can be considered to be accepting and no contract exists.[13]

1.3.3 Termination of an offer

An offer can be terminated in various ways:

Revocation

This refers to withdrawing an offer at any time before acceptance takes place.[14] A fundamental rule is that revocation must be communicated to the offeree before acceptance.[15] Revocation by a third party is valid as long as the offeror has shown a clear intention to revoke their offer by words or conduct, regardless of the means of communication.[16]

9 *Payne v Cave* [1789] 3 Term Rep 148; S57(2) Sale of Goods Act 1979.
10 *Spencer v Harding* [1870] LR 5 CP 561.
11 *Harvela Investment Ltd v Royal Trust Canada Ltd* [1986] AC 207.
12 *Taylor v Laird* (1865) 25 LJ Ex 329.
13 See *Tinn v Hoffman* [1873] 29 LT 271.
14 *Routledge v Grant* [1828] 4 Bing 653.
15 *Byrne v Van Tienhoven* 1880 5 CPD 344.
16 *Dickinson v Dodds* [1876] 2 CH D 463.

A unilateral offer can be revoked by using the same means of communication in which the offer was made.[17] However, revocation of a unilateral offer can cause particular difficulties. Once the offeree has embarked on performing the required act, the offeror cannot prevent the offeree from completing the act. It is therefore nearly impossible to revoke an offer in unilateral contracts once the offeree has embarked on performing the required act.[18]

Lapse of time

After the passage of time, the offer will no longer remain alive and is therefore ineffective and not capable of acceptance.[19] An offer might contain within in it a time limit for acceptance; if it does not, the court will consider the offer to lapse after a "reasonable time".

Death

In cases of an offer of a contract relating to personal services, death of a party is likely to terminate the offer which is therefore not capable of a valid acceptance. However, in other cases, especially where the offeree is not aware of the offeror's death, the offeror can still be bound.[20]

Non-compliance with a condition

This refers to the non-fulfilment of a condition, also known as a condition precedent. An offer can be terminated if the parties have not met those conditions. Therefore, in practice, the offer is incapable of being accepted on the conditions agreed.[21] For example, the offer to sell a business might be conditional on the buyer first providing proof of funds.

1.4 Acceptance

For there to be a valid contract, the acceptance must exactly match the terms of the offer, also known as the "mirror image" rule. If the acceptance is qualified in any way and does not match the terms of the offer, it will not be a valid acceptance.

1.4.1 Counteroffers

Varying the terms of the offer may amount to a counteroffer or a request for further information. The distinction between the two legal principles is important, as the legal consequences will often depend on the facts. The effect of a counterof-

17 *Shuey v United States* (1875) 92 US 73.
18 See *Daulia Ltd v Four Millbank Nominees Limited and Another* [1978] 2 WLR 621; *Errington v Errington* [1952] 1 KB 290.
19 *Ramsgate Victoria Hotel Co Ltd v Montefiore* (1866) LR 1 Ex 109.
20 See *Bradbury v Morgan* (1861) 1 H&C 249 for an example.
21 *Financing Ltd v Stimson* [1962] 1 WLR 1184.

fer is that the original offer is extinguished, and the new counteroffer remains open for acceptance.

Consider this scenario

Xian offers to sell his smartphone for £250. Kiera tells Xian that it is too expensive and offers Xian £150 instead. Kiera then changes her mind and agrees to buy the smartphone for £250. Can the original offer of £250 be accepted?

In this scenario, the original offer of £250 is extinguished and Kiera's new offer of £150 is a valid offer capable of acceptance. Therefore, as Xian's offer of £250 is extinguished, it cannot be accepted by Kiera; it has been destroyed and is therefore incapable of acceptance. If Xian accepts Kiera's counteroffer of £150, then an agreement has been reached provided that all the other requirements have been met (consideration, intention to create legal relations, and capacity).[22]

1.4.2 Difficulties with standard form contracts and counteroffers

Issues can arise when contracting on standard terms, such as a dispute on whose terms prevail, and whether the contract was made on the offeror's terms. This is known as the "battle of the forms" and the "last shot doctrine" where the parties are in dispute as to whose terms apply if each of their terms differ.[23] The courts' approach to this is that the terms that prevail are those of the person who gets the last shot, i.e. the last party to send their terms before the other party begins performing the contract.[24]

1.4.3 Request for further information or mere inquiry

In certain circumstances, the offer will remain open. This is the case where the response is a request for further information. Where the offeree requests more information, this does not alter the terms of the offer. Clarifying the exact terms of the offer will not amount to an attempt to change the terms of an offer; therefore, the offer remains alive. Requests for further information, such as "Will the car be the same price if it is sold with the extra set of wheels you have?" will generally have no effect or impact on the original offer as there is no attempt to change the original terms of the offer.[25]

22 This is best illustrated in the case of *Hyde v Wrench* (1840) 3 Beav 334, 49 ER 132, where the original offer was destroyed, and because of this, the original was no longer capable of acceptance.

23 Lord Denning in *Butler Machine Tool Co Ltd v Ex-Cell-O Corporation Limited* [1979] 1 WLR 401. This is the leading case where it was held that the buyer's order amounted to a counteroffer and therefore the contract was concluded on the buyer's terms and not the seller's terms.

24 *Butler Machine Tool Co Ltd v Ex-Cell-O Corporation Limited* [1979] 1 WLR 401.

25 See *Stevenson, Jaques & Co v McLean* (1880) 5 QBD 346.

1.4.4 Communication of acceptance

As seen in the previous chapter, the person accepting the offer must be aware of the offer. In turn, the offeree must communicate their acceptance to the offeror. The person communicating the acceptance must have the authority to do so; this can be a third party.[26] The general rule is that acceptance must be communicated; silence does not amount to acceptance.[27] However, some exceptions to this rule are outlined below.

Acceptance by conduct

An offeror's conduct can amount to acceptance despite their silence in some cases.[28] For example, when a customer brings goods to the till in a shop, scanning the goods and asking for payment might amount to acceptance on behalf of the cashier. The courts will consider in the circumstances whether the conduct reasonably amounts to acceptance.

Acceptance by performance

In unilateral contracts, the offeree's conduct of performing the required act constitutes acceptance. In these circumstances, communication is waived by conduct, for example, responding to a notice for a reward of £100 for anyone who finds my lost black-and-white dog, Barney. Returning Barney will be the act, and so long as the offeree returns Barney, the offeree will be entitled to the £100. The act of looking for and finding the dog is the acceptance by conduct. As noted above, it is generally considered to not be possible to revoke an unilateral offer once the offeree has begun performance of the required act.

It is also possible to accept a bilateral offer by beginning to perform the contract under its terms. For example, by driving into a paid car park and parking your car, you are accepting the offer to park on the terms imposed by the car park operator.

Acceptance by performance is often present in cases where the "last shot rule" applies, which is explained later in this chapter.

Acceptance through post: the postal rule

Another exception to the rule that silence does not amount to a valid acceptance is the "postal rule". Acceptance takes place as soon as the letter is posted. The acceptance does not need to be actually communicated to the offeror to be deemed a valid acceptance, provided it is properly addressed and posted. However, the post must be a reasonable or anticipated means of a valid acceptance (dis-

26 *Powell v Lee* [1908] 99 LT 284.

27 For the general rule that silence cannot amount to acceptance, see the leading case of *Felthouse v Bindley* (1862) 11 CBNS 869, 142 ER 1037 and *Entores v Miles Far East Corporation* [1955] 2 QB 327 concerning instantaneous methods of communication.

28 *Brogden v Metropolitan Railway Co* [1877] 2 App Cas 666.

cussed later). In some cases, the postal rule can be ousted by stipulating that actual communication is required.[29]

Instantaneous methods of communication

Since the postal rule, communication technology has advanced. It must be noted that the postal rule only applies to the post. During a face-to-face interaction, it is relatively straightforward to establish whether there has been a valid acceptance and the point at which a valid contract had been formed. However, difficulties arise with different forms of instantaneous methods as they may not be accessed instantly. This therefore creates issues in terms of deciphering whether there is a valid acceptance.[30] These methods include telex, fax, email, text, messaging systems used on virtual office platforms, telephone, traditional answering machines, and voicemail messages. The general rule is that acceptance must be communicated, in other words, the receipt rule applies – acceptance takes place when it is received by the party who made the offer. At what point acceptance takes place can, however, be debatable.

Consider the following scenario:

> Lola runs a flower shop and wants to order a batch of tulips from Winston, a regular supplier of tulip flowers. On 1 May Lola emails Winston offering to purchase a batch of tulips for £300. Lola stipulates that she would like acknowledgment by 7 May. Winston receives the email and responds on 4 May. However, due to a problem with Lola's email provider, Lola does not receive the email until 8 May. When will the acceptance be valid according to the receipt rule?

Following the receipt rule the acceptance will be deemed valid when the email is available to be read by Lola on 8 May although Winston sent the email on 4 May. Therefore, the contract will not come into force until 8 May, not 4 May when Winston responded. On the other hand, consider the position where the email was sent on 4 May and arrives in Lola's inbox instantly but Lola's laptop is broken, so she does not check her email until 8 May. In this scenario the contract would be made on 4 May as the email was "received" and was available to be read. This

29 For authority on this area, see *Adams v Lindsell* [1818] 1 B & Ald 681; *Re London Northern Bank, ex p. Jones* [1900] 1 Ch 220 on the principle that it has to be properly posted; *Henthorn v Fraser* [1892] 2 Ch 27 on whether post is reasonable or anticipated means of a valid acceptance; *Household Fire and Carriage Accident Insurance Co. v Grant* [1879] 4 Ex D 216 on avoidance of the postal rule in cases where communication is required. On expressly ousting the postal rule, see *Holwell Securities v Hughes* [1974] 1 WLR 155.

30 See *Brinkibon v Stahag Stahl* [1983] 2 AC 34, where Lord Wilberforce said, "No universal rule can cover all such cases; they must be resolved by reference to the intentions of the parties, by sound business practice and in some cases by a judgement where the risks should lie." See also *Entores v Miles Far East Corporation* [1955] 2 QB 327 concerning the receipt rule, i.e., acceptance must be received or communicated.

creates problems and uncertainty when dealing with acceptance in terms of instantaneous methods of communication.

Various situations are outlined below where this is not always clear:

- *Acceptance sent within office hours*: If acceptance of an offer made in a commercial context occurs within office hours, it is deemed to be a valid acceptance. The reasoning behind this is that the offeree has taken all reasonable steps to ensure the acceptance is communicated.[31]
- *Acceptance sent outside office hours*: Outside office hours, acceptance is deemed to take place at the start of the next working day when the recipient could reasonably have been expected to read it.[32]
- *Where does the fault lie?* It is the responsibility of the offeree to ensure that their acceptance is received. However, this is not always easy to decipher.[33]

1.4.5 Specified mode of acceptance prescribed

In most cases, the offeree is generally free to accept the offer in the manner they wish. However, where the offeror stipulates the prescribed mode, any acceptance that does not adhere to that prescribed mode will not be valid. This can be waived if it benefits the offeree as long as the offeror is not put at a disadvantage.[34]

31 *Tenax Steamship Co Limited v The Brimnes (Owners) (The Brimnes)* [1975] QB 929.

32 *Mondial Shipping and Chartering BV v Astarte Shipping Limited* [1995] CLC 1011. See, obiter, *Thomas v BPE Solicitors* [2010] EWHC 206 (Ch) for what constitutes office hours, dependent on the type of business and hours of operation.

33 *Entores v Miles Far East Corporation* [1955] 2 QB 327. Look at Lord Denning's examples of cases that relate to fault. Lord Denning uses the example of two people shouting across from opposite sides of a river, trying to accept an offer. This highlights the issue of whether the acceptance has been successfully communicated, and if not, it should be repeated.

34 *Yates Building Co. Limited v Pulleyn & Sons (York) Limited* [1975] 119 SJ 370. See also *Tinn v Hoffman & Co* [1873] 29 LT 271. In this case, the offeror stipulated post.

Chapter 1 Revision Points

Types of contract

- Unilateral
- Bilateral

Offer

- Distinguish from invitation to treat
- Advertisements
- Display of goods
- Auctions
- Tenders
- Termination of an offer
- Revocation
- Lapse of time
- Death
- Non-compliance with a condition

Acceptance

- General rule – must be communicated
- Exceptions/rules
- Counteroffer or request for further information
- Conduct
- Unilateral contracts
- Postal rule
- Instantaneous methods of communication

It is important to check your knowledge using the following Multiple Choice Questions.

Multiple Choice Questions

Question 1

Syreeta, Leyla, and Rachel attend an auction. The auctioneer invites bids for a unique Cotex watch. Syreeta bids £1,000. Another person at the auction bids £1,500 and the auctioneer accepts this bid. The next item to be auctioned is a rare brooch. Leyla is indecisive and raises her hand slightly. There are no higher bids. The auctioneer states, "Sold to Leyla for £350". Shortly after, Leyla decides that she does not want the brooch.

Which of the following best describes the legal position?

A. There is no contract between the auctioneer and Syreeta, as acceptance has not taken place. Leyla has potentially formed a contract based on the objective approach.

B. There is a contract between the auctioneer and Syreeta, as acceptance has taken place. Leyla has potentially formed a contract based on the objective approach.

C. There is no contract between the auctioneer and Syreeta, as acceptance has not taken place. There is no contract between Leyla and the auctioneer based on the objective approach.

D. There is no contract between the auctioneer and Syreeta, as acceptance has not taken place. Leyla has potentially formed a contract based on the subjective approach.

E. There is a contract between the auctioneer and Syreeta, as acceptance has taken place. There is no contract between Leyla and the auctioneer based on the subjective approach.

Question 2

Stephanie has decided to open a local coffee shop. Stephanie places an advert in the *Bush Chronicle*, which states, "Coffee R Us is offering ten free subscriptions which entitle the winners to two cups of coffee or tea every week for six months to the first ten people who arrive at 10 am to purchase coffee on Sunday". On Sunday, Stephanie has a large queue outside her coffee shop. As she did not expect so many customers, she decides to give away the free subscription to only the first five customers instead of the first ten. There are five other customers who arrived at 10 am and purchased a coffee complaining they are entitled to the free coffee membership.

Which of the following best describes the legal position?

A. There is a bilateral contract accepted by conduct, as the five customers have promised to arrive at Coffee R Us at 10 am and buy the coffee.
B. There is a unilateral contract accepted by communication, as the five customers have accepted a valid offered by communicating their intention to perform.
C. There is no unilateral contract accepted by conduct, as the five customers have not accepted a valid offer by performance.
D. There is a unilateral contract accepted by conduct as the five customers have accepted a valid offer by performance, by arriving at Coffee R Us at 10 am and buying the coffee.
E. There is no contract formed because the five customers did not promise in advance to arrive at Coffee R Us at 10 am and buy the coffee.

Question 3

Hamid decides to sell his limited-edition Porta 911 4s Turbo. Hamid places an advertisement on a used car website: "*Porta* 911 *4s Turbo excellent condition, with one owner* £25,000 *or the nearest offer. Please contact Hamid on* 078345678 *(evening) or* 028041124 *(during office hours 9–5 pm)*".

On 3 July, Uche calls Hamid's mobile number (after inspecting the vehicle the previous day) and offers £23,500. Hamid says "How about £24,500?" Uche states that she will need to discuss this with her husband. Hamid tells her to call back at 6 pm. Uche contacts Hamid by phone at 7:30 pm; however, his phone has no reception. Uche tries Hamid's work number the following day (4 July) but receives no answer, so she leaves a message on the answering machine stating that she wants the Porta 911 4s Turbo for £24,500. Hamid does not get to the office until late that afternoon and does not access any messages that day. Uche then tries his mobile in the evening, but it still does not have reception. Uche contacts Hamid the following day, demanding the vehicle for the advertised price. Unfortunately, the car has been sold.

Which of the following best describes the legal position?

A. Hamid's advert is an offer. Uche has made a valid counteroffer of £23,500, which is clear, certain, communicated, and capable of acceptance. There is a further counteroffer of £24,500 made by Hamid. It would be reasonable, and Hamid's responsibility to check his answering machine on that day, and therefore a contract is formed on 4 July.

B. Hamid's advert is an invitation to treat. Uche has made a valid offer of £23,500, which is clear, certain, communicated, and capable of acceptance. There is a counteroffer of £24,500 made by Hamid. It would be reasonable, and Hamid's responsibility to check his answering machine on that day. Therefore, a contract is formed on 4 July.

C. Hamid's advert is an invitation to treat. Uche has made a valid offer of £23,500, which is clear, certain, communicated, and capable of acceptance. There is a counteroffer of £24,500 made by Hamid. It would be Uche's responsibility to check that Hamid has received the message; therefore, a contract has not been formed.

D. Hamid's advert is an invitation to treat. Uche has made a valid offer of £23,500, which is clear, certain, communicated, and capable of acceptance. There is a counteroffer of £24,500 made by Hamid. It would not be reasonable for Hamid to check his answering machine until the next day, and therefore a contract is formed on 5 July.

E. Hamid's advert is a unilateral offer. Uche has accepted that unilateral offer by making a valid offer of £23,500, which is clear, certain, communicated, and capable of acceptance. There is a contract formed at that point.

2 Intention to create legal relations, certainty, and capacity

2.1 Chapter overview

This chapter focuses on the intention to create legal relations, certainty, and capacity as essential elements in the formation of a contract. A fundamental legal principle is that where there is no intention to be legally bound, or a lack of certainty, or capacity, a valid contract will not be present. The chapter will emphasise the rebuttable presumptions used when deciding whether there is an intention to create legal relations in commercial and domestic contexts. The chapter will distinguish between the logical formation rules relating to various contexts in determining intention and certainty. In addition, it will focus on contracts with minors, individuals lacking mental capacity, and corporations.

2.2 Intention to create legal relations

Intention is a fundamental legal principle in ascertaining whether a contract is legally binding and thus has legal repercussions or ramifications in the event of a breach. Where the agreement lacks this, there will be no contract. The courts adopt an objective approach in determining intention by the actions of the parties that involves analysing the situation as an objective observer rather than inquiring into what was in the parties' minds.[1] The law uses presumptions to divide agreements into commercial or social and domestic agreements to determine whether intention is present (see Figure 2.1).

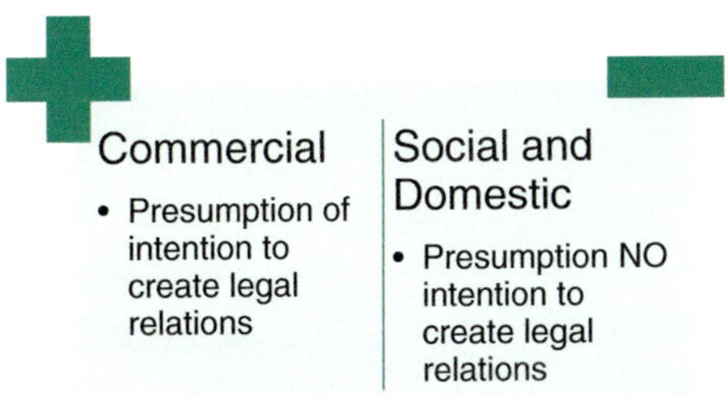

Figure 2.1 Intention to create legal relations

1 *Edmonds v Lawson* [2000] QB 501 (CA) per Bingham LJ.

DOI: 10.4324/9781032642161-4

2.2.1 Social and domestic agreements

In social and domestic contexts, the presumption is that the parties do not intend to create legal relations unless there is clear evidence to the contrary. This presumption is logical in these circumstances as the disagreements in these contexts (such as meeting for a family meal or agreeing to do a spring clean as a favour for a family member) may relate to social and domestic arrangements, where the parties would generally not intend to sue for not adhering to the agreement or obligations.[2] Consider this scenario:

> Shakira and Jack have been married for over 10 years with 3 children. Jack has been a partner in a well-known West End solicitor's firm for over 3 years and works long hours. Shakira constantly complains that she is fed up with being at home with the children, so they both decide to take a break with the intention of saving the marriage. They agreed that Jack would sleep in the room downstairs for a few months and stay at his parents' house on the weekends. Jack promises to pay Shakira £1,500 per month "to cover the bills" until they decide the best way forward to save the marriage. Three months later Jack meets Sianna and falls in love with her and stops paying the maintenance. Shakira finds this out from her best friend Susan, and threatens Jack with legal proceedings to which Jack responds "see you in court". Is the promise to pay the £1,500 enforceable?[3]

It is clear that this is a domestic arrangement as it is between a wife and husband, therefore the rebuttable presumption applies in that there is no legal intention to create a legal relationship. They were both still married at the time of the agreement. On the facts this presumption has not been rebutted as there is no evidence to the contrary. The agreement to pay the £1,500 will lack intention, and therefore, this promise will be unenforceable.

What if the couple were separating and seeking legal advice about divorce proceedings when making this arrangement?[4]

Clearly this would change the legal advice. There would be clear evidence to rebut the presumption as it would be clear that both parties did not intend to live amicably, and therefore, the agreement would be enforceable and not lack legal intent.

Therefore clear evidence of an intention to create legal relations will rebut the presumption. Such evidence might include committing the contract to writing (and other formalities such as signing the agreement), one party relying on the contract

2 See *Jones v Padavatton* [1968] EWCA Civ 4 for an example of this where a contract between mother and daughter was held to not be made with the intention to create legal relations.

3 *Balfour v Balfour* [1919] 2 KB 571.

4 *Merritt v Merritt* [1970] 1 WLR 1211.

to their detriment, or that the agreement contained "mutuality" in that all parties made similar promises to one another. For example, playing the National Lottery with a group of friends (also known as a syndicate) and promising any individual who wins will share the prize money is evidence that the agreement has the requisite intention to be legally binding. In cases such as these, the presumed intention not to be bound will be rebutted.[5]

2.2.2 Commercial agreements

If an express agreement is concluded in a commercial context, it is presumed that the parties intend to create a legal relationship unless there is strong evidence to the contrary. Context is important in deciding whether the presumption has been rebutted.[6] These rules apply to agreements between businesses and agreements between a business and an individual. In order to rebut the presumption, the party asserting that there was no intention would be legally bound to prove this. In determining whether the presumption has been rebutted, the courts look at the words used.[7] To rebut the presumption, clear words must be used; otherwise, it is unlikely that the presumption will be rebutted.[8] In some cases, the courts have decided that in a commercial context, an intention to create a legal relationship did not exist. For example, the term "subject to contract" allows parties to seek further information or even advice without being legally bound by the contract.

Letters of comfort

It is of particular importance to note the legal consequences of a letter of comfort to provide reassurance in the commercial context as the law is not clear in terms of its legal significance. Letters of comfort are usually used to provide assurance in cases where the borrower is obtaining a loan, and the lender requests a reassurance that the borrower is capable of paying back the debt and obligations under the agreement. Regardless of the name of the document, it is important to look at the context of the agreement in terms of the wording of the letter as normally these letters will not be contractually binding.[9]

5 See *Simpkins v Pays* [1955] 1 WLR 975.

6 See *Edwards v Skyways Ltd* [1969] 1 WLR 349 for an example of the importance of language concerning *ex gratia*.

7 In some cases, intent is not clear. In *Esso Petroleum v Customs and Excise Commissioners* [1976] 1 All ER 117, it was held that the coins used in a sales promotion had not rebutted the presumption in a commercial context because the coins generated business and a commercial benefit from the World Cup coins.

8 *Rose & Frank Co. v JR Crompton Bros* [1923] 2 KB 261, but compare *Esso Petroleum Ltd v Customs & Excise Commissioners* [1976] 1 WLR 117, where the courts concluded that because Esso was trying to generate more business from the promotion, there was intention.

9 See *Kleinwort Benson Ltd v Malaysia Mining Corporation Bhd* [1989] 1 WLR 379 for an example of this.

2.3 Certainty

In determining whether a contract exists or whether an agreement has been reached, the terms must not be vague.[10] This will ensure that both parties understand what they are agreeing to and their obligations under the contract. For an agreement to be complete, the terms must be certain for it to have contractual force and be legally enforceable. The law has taken an objective test to determine this.[11]

For certainty to exist:

- Terms must not be vague or ambiguous;
- The terms must be definite and clear;
- The terms should be able to be enforced by the court; if not, the court may conclude that there was no agreement in place when the parties contracted together;
- Both parties need to have the same interpretation of the terms contained in the contract.

Consider this scenario:

> Austin, a carpenter, contracts with Amel to lay wooden flooring throughout her house. As part of the contract, they both agree the following (main clause taken from the contract):
>
> > Austin Marshall agrees to supply and lay brown 6mm wooden flooring in Amel's entire house: at 10 Hepton Close, London W123 9TT. Austin will commence work on 1 July and complete by 10 July. The cost of the work will be £10,000 including VAT to be paid in two instalments. Amel will pay £5,000 on 5 July and £5,000 on 10 July (on completion of the work).

Will the courts consider this clause in the contract certain and are the terms clear?

It is clear that the terms contained in this clause are not vague as:

- The parties are clearly named;
- The work to be carried out is clearly stated (to lay brown 6mm wooden flooring);
- The commencement and end date are clearly set out above;
- The cost of the work, service, and goods is clearly set out above.

The contract ensures that there is not much room for disagreement and vagueness, therefore it is highly likely that the courts will enforce this agreement if there is any dispute between the parties.

10 See *Scammell v Ouston* [1941] AC 251, where it was held that the wording "on hire purchase" was uncertain and therefore too vague to be enforceable. See also *Hillas v Arcos* (1932) 147 LT 503 for an example where the agreement was binding.

11 *RTS Flexible Systems Ltd v Molkerei Alois Müller GmbH & Company KG (UK Production)* [2010] UKSC 14.

2.4 Capacity

In determining whether a contract exists, capacity is essential. If a party to the contract lacks capacity, it may not be legally enforceable. Therefore, the parties might be unable to enforce any potential legal rights they may have under it. To ensure that the agreement is legally enforceable, and parties can sue under the contract, the legal standing of the parties is important. Therefore, parties who wish to enforce their legal rights under a contract must have full capacity. Generally, adults (those over 18) have full capacity to contract. However, there are some exceptional situations which will be considered in the following subsections.

2.4.1 Minors

The law has restricted the capacity of minors to enter valid contracts to protect them as they are regarded in law as vulnerable. Contracts with minors are generally unenforceable. The other party is bound, meaning that the minor can enforce the contract against the other party, but the other party cannot assert their legal rights against the minor. However, exceptions to this rule in certain transactions with a minor include contracts for necessaries that are essential for survival.[12] These necessaries can include goods and services. In determining what is necessary for the minor, the law considers the minor's social status in society.[13] The law also realises that minors may enter "beneficial" contracts that are of benefit to their ability to prepare themselves for a future career, such as employment, education, training, and apprenticeships. In these cases, generally, where the minor contracts for necessaries or for beneficial education, training, or employment it is enforceable by both parties unless the contract is oppressive.[14]

2.4.2 Mental capacity and intoxication

If an individual does not have the capacity or is drunk at the time of entering a contract, the contract is deemed voidable if it is proven that the individual did not understand the nature of the transaction and the other party was aware of the situation.[15] It goes without saying that if they understood the nature of the transaction, the contract would not be voidable.

2.4.3 Corporations

Corporations are legal entities and have separate legal identities that separate them from the individuals who have formed the corporation. A company, for example, forms contracts as a legal person separate from the company's

12 *Nash v Inman* [1908] 2 KB 1.
13 See S3(3) The Sale of Goods Act 1979, where necessaries are defined as "goods suitable to the condition in life of the minor and to his actual requirements at the time of sale and delivery".
14 For examples, see *De Francesco v Barnum* [1890] 45 ChD 430 and *Proform Sports Management Ltd v Proactive Sports Management* [2006] EWHC 2903.
15 See SS1(2), 2, 3(1), 3(4), and 7 Mental Capacity Act 2005 for further details about the capacity to enter contracts.

shareholders. This means that a company can sue in its own name, and will be sued in its own name, which provides a level of legal protection for the people who formed and work for the company.

Chapter 2 Revision Points

Intention to create legal relations

- Rebuttable presumptions
- Social and domestic agreements (presumption: intention to create legal relations)
- Commercial agreements (presumption: no intention to create legal relations)

Certainty

- Courts take an objective test
- Terms must not be vague or ambiguous
- Terms must be clear and interpreted the same by both parties

Capacity

- Minors
- Mental intoxication
- Corporations

It is important to check your knowledge using the following Multiple Choice Questions.

Multiple Choice Questions

Question 1

Melissa is a qualified tax accountant. During a family dinner, her brother Raymond tells Melissa that he has been having some difficulties completing his annual tax return. Melissa tells Raymond that she would be happy to "take a look". Melissa writes down in her diary that she will help Raymond with his tax return and that Raymond will pay her £200. Both Melissa and Raymond sign the diary page. The next day, Melissa visits Raymond at home and helps him complete his tax return. Raymond now refuses to pay the £200.

Which of the following best describes the legal position?

A. This is a commercial agreement. The rebuttable presumption is that there is an intention to create legal relations. The presumption has been rebutted because they are siblings and therefore, the promise to pay Raymond £200 is not enforceable.
B. This is a commercial agreement, as it is Melissa's business. The rebuttable presumption is that there is intention to create legal relations; therefore, the promise to pay Raymond £200 is enforceable.
C. This is a social/domestic agreement. The rebuttable presumption is that there is no intention to create legal relations. The presumption has not been rebutted, and, therefore, the agreement to pay Raymond £200 is not enforceable.
D. This is a social/domestic agreement, and there is an irrebuttable presumption that it will not be legally enforceable. Raymond is not entitled to the £200 .
E. This is a social/domestic agreement. The rebuttable presumption is that there is no intention to create legal relations. The presumption has been rebutted as the agreement is in writing.

Question 2

Eden is 17 and has just inherited over £10,000 from her late grandparents. She decides to purchase a new top-of-the-range ITablet for £500 from Tablets R Us, an electronics store. Shortly after the purchase, Eden realises that she has a similar ITablet at home. The only thing that is different is the camera and not the operating system. Eden returns the ITablet to Tablets R Us. The duty manager refuses to accept her return because the item has been opened.

Which of the following best describes the legal position?

A. The ITablet is likely to be classified as necessaries, and therefore the contract is not voidable. Eden has the discretion to cancel the contract.

B. The ITablet is likely to be classified as necessaries, and therefore the contract is not voidable. Eden does not have the discretion to cancel the contract.

C. The ITablet is unlikely to be classified as necessaries, and therefore the contract is voidable. Eden has the discretion to cancel the contract and can argue that it is not enforceable against her.

D. The ITablet is unlikely to be classified as necessaries, and therefore the contract is void. Eden has the discretion to cancel the contract.

E. The contract is voidable, and it does not matter whether the goods are classified as necessaries.

3 Consideration

3.1 Chapter overview

For a contract to be legal, it must involve consideration. Without consideration, there is no contract, and therefore the contract will not be enforceable. This chapter will focus on the traditional requirements for consideration, the legal principles used to determine whether consideration is present in forming a contract, the need for further consideration in terms of altering promises, and existing contractual obligations and promises to pay more and pay less. This chapter will also cover the equitable exception to the traditional rule of consideration, promissory estoppel.

3.2 What is consideration?

Put simply, consideration is the price paid in exchange for the promise of the other party.[1] Another way to define consideration is as some right, interest, profit, or benefit accruing to the promisee (the party to whom the promise is being made) or some forbearance, detriment, loss, or responsibility given, suffered, or undertaken by the promisor (the party making the promise).[2]

For example, if A buys a coffee at a coffee shop from B for £3.00, A gains the coffee, cup, and lid but loses the £3.00, while B loses the coffee, cup, and lid but gains the £3.00.

3.2.1 Executed and executory consideration

Executory consideration is often referred to as the situation of a promise to do something that involves a promise and exchange. The performance comes later; in other words, it has not happened yet, whereas executed consideration refers to a situation where the performance for the exchange is carried out at the same time as the agreement. Take, for example, a situation where A offers £500 for the return of their lost dog, Bunny. If B brings back the lost dog in response to the offer being communicated to B, B's consideration would be executed as B would have

1 *Dunlop v Selfridge* [1915] AC 847.
2 *Currie v Misa* [1875] LR 10 EX 153.

DOI: 10.4324/9781032642161-5

completed the required act or bargain, constituting acceptance by performance. The liability to pay will be on the other side, in this case, A.[3] This will amount to executed consideration.

3.2.2 Consideration must move from the promisee

Consideration must move from the promisee; this means that consideration must be provided by the party to the contract, not a third party. Otherwise, the party that has not provided consideration cannot bring an action as they have failed to provide any consideration for the promise, a fundamental principle in contract law.[4] This is linked to the doctrine of privity of contract discussed in Chapter 4 in that those who are parties to the contract must provide consideration.

3.2.3 Past consideration

The general rule is that past consideration is not good consideration and therefore under law will mean that there will not be a binding contract. Past consideration is an act that has already been done at the time the promisor promises to do it. A fundamental rule is that consideration must be given in exchange. The act or promise must be carried out in return for the promise made. If the act being relied on as consideration has already taken place before the promise has been carried out, this will amount to past consideration, and therefore, is not legally valid consideration.[5] However, an exception to the past consideration rule is where performance of the act was requested by the other party before it was carried out.[6] This is sometimes referred to using the Latin phrase *implied assumpsit* (see Figure 3.1).

3.2.4 Sufficiency versus adequacy

Consideration need not be adequate but must be sufficient.[7] It cannot be vague but must be substantial in the context.[8] The courts are not concerned with the adequacy of consideration (whether the exchange represents fair value) but are rather concerned with the sufficiency of consideration, which means that consideration must have some economic value in the eyes of the law. This applies even when consideration has little economic value.[9] For example, if I sell my Bentley worth £130,000 (market value) to X for £1,000, the court is not interested

3 See *Carlill v Carbolic Smoke Ball Co* [1893] 1 QB 256 for an example of this.

4 See *Tweddle v Atkinson* [1861] 1 B & S 393.

5 In *Roscorla v Thomas* (1842) 3 QB 234, the assurance that the horse was "sound and free from vice" was given after the sale, and therefore amounted to past consideration, which in law, was not good consideration. See also *Re McArdle* [1951] Ch 669 and *Eastwood v Kenyon* [1840] 11 Ad & El 438 (QB) for other examples of past consideration.

6 For the application of requested performance, see *Re Casey's Patents* [1892] 1 Ch 104 and Lord Scarman in *Pao On v Lau Yiu Long* [1980] AC 614.

7 For an example of sufficiency, see *Thomas v Thomas* [1842] 2 QB 851.

8 For examples of where moral obligations are love and affection, not to nag is too vague to amount to consideration. See *Eastwood v Kenyon* [1840] 11 AD & E1 438 and *White v Bluett* [1853] 23 LJ Ex 36.

9 For an example of where chocolate wrappers had very little economic value but were still sufficient consideration, see *Chappell & Co. Ltd v Nestlé Co Ltd* [1960] 2 All ER 701.

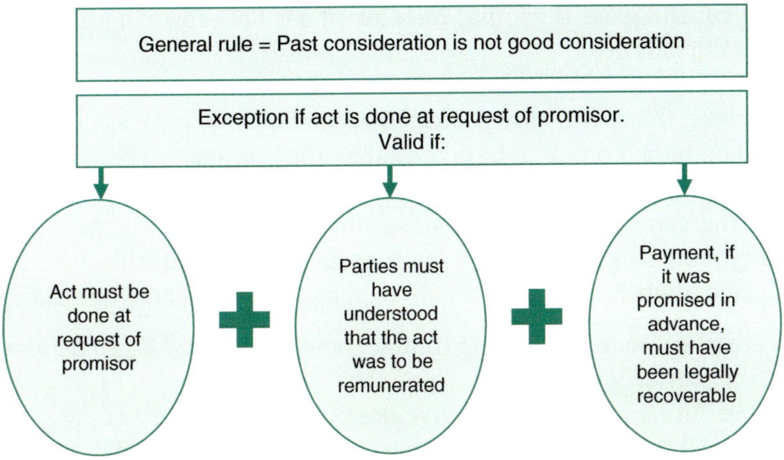

Figure 3.1 The *implied assumpsit* exception

in the price paid; they are only interested in whether there was any consideration. There is consideration (the payment of £1,000), so there is a valid agreement. This supports the idea of freedom in a contract: Both parties should be able to make their bargain without the interference of the court concerning whether it sufficiently benefits them.

3.3 Existing duties and consideration

3.3.1 Existing public duties

Performing an existing public duty will not amount to sufficient or good consideration unless the person is going above and beyond their public duty. For example, a police officer offered extra money to stop a criminal for stealing someone's bag does not have a contractual right to the reward, because they are only offering their existing public duty as consideration. This will not be enforceable as the police are already under a public duty and required by law to arrest suspects or criminals. However, going beyond this, for example, by requesting police presence at a private function or to ensure a football match is safe would amount to sufficient consideration.[10]

3.3.2 Existing contractual duties

It is well established in contract law that if person A is already under a contractual duty to do something for person B, they cannot use that duty as fresh consideration.[11] Therefore if I promise to cut your grass for £20, I cannot then agree with you

10 *Glasbrook Bros v Glamorgan County Council* [1925] AC 270 is an example of doing something extra or going over and beyond a public duty.
11 Compare *Stilk v Myrick* [1809] 2 Camp 317 with *Hartley v Ponsonby* [1857] 7 El & Bl 872.

that I will cut the grass if you pay me £30 – I am not promising to do anything more than I already owe.

In recent cases, the courts have been creative and gone to great lengths in finding consideration for a promise to be enforceable. The principle of "practical benefit"[12] has been recognised and refined to allow the court to look at the commercial reality of the contract. Where one party obtains a "practical benefit" from the other party promising to perform an existing contractual duty, this may constitute good consideration. For practical benefit to apply, the guidelines state that:

- There needs to be an existing contract between the parties to perform a service or provide goods;
- The performing party has given notice or informed the other party that they are unable to perform unless extra payment is given without duress or fraud;
- There is a practical benefit gained from the completion of the contract.

For example, a company might be willing to pay a contractor more to complete a contract that the contractor will otherwise breach, because it avoids the company suffering a greater loss if the work is not done.

An existing contractual duty owed to a third party can also amount to good consideration.[13]

3.3.3 Agreements to accept a lesser sum

The general rule concerning payments to accept a lesser sum (part payment of a debt) is not good consideration because the debtor is not promising to do anything more than they are already obliged to do (pay the creditor).[14] This is also known as a part payment of debt. Common law exceptions to this rule are:

- Payment of a lesser sum at the creditor's request before the sum is due;
- Payment by a different method;
- Payment at a different place than originally agreed;
- Payment by a third party.[15]

The principle that a "practical benefit" might be good consideration when varying an existing contract as demonstrated in *Williams v Roffey Bros*[16] does not apply for payments to accept less.[17]

12 *Williams v Roffey Bros* [1991] 1 QB 1.
13 See *Scotson v Pegg* [1861] 6 H & N 296.
14 *Pinnel's Case* [1602] 5 Co Rep 117a and *Foakes v Beer* [1884] 9 App Cas 605.
15 *Welby v Drake* (1825) 1 C & P 557.
16 *Williams v Roffey Bros* [1991] 1 QB 1.
17 See *Re Selectmove Ltd* [1995] 1 WLR 474 and *MWB Business Exchange Centres Ltd v Rock Advertising Ltd* [2018] UKSC 24.

3.4 Promissory estoppel

Promissory estoppel is an equitable exception to the rule of part payment that can be raised as a defence but cannot be used to bring a cause of action. In other words, the person must wait to be sued and then raise it as a defence; it operates in the absence of consideration and has strict parameters in terms of relying on the doctrine as a defence.[18]

1 It can only be used as a defence, in other words, as a shield and not a sword. Otherwise, the defence will fail;
2 There must be a clear and unequivocal promise to waive strict legal rights;
3 The promisee must have altered their position, although this does not have to be to the detriment of the promisee;
4 The promisee can only rely on the doctrine if they have "clean hands", and it must be inequitable for the promisor to go back on their promise;
5 Any relief under the doctrine is discretionary.

In most cases, the effect of the estoppel will only be to suspend the rights of the other party, not extinguish them entirely, and that party can restore their rights by giving reasonable notice to the other party.[19] For example, a landlord might promise to only ask for half of the usual amount of rent from their tenant while their tenant is ill and unable to work, but when the tenant returns to health the landlord can give notice that the rent will return to the original amount.

18 *Central London Property Trust v High Trees* [1947] KB 130.
19 *Tool Metal Manufacturing Co Ltd v Tungsten Electric Co Ltd* [1955] 1 WLR 761.

Chapter 3 Revision Points

Consideration

- Executed and executory consideration
- Rules
  - Must move from promise
  - Past consideration
  - Sufficiency versus adequacy
  - Existing public and contractual duties
  - Payments to accept a lesser sum (part payment of debts)
- Equitable discretionary exception to common law rules: promissory estoppel requirements
  - Shield not a sword
  - Clear and unequivocal promise
  - Promisee must have altered their position
  - Inequitable for the promisor to go back on their promise

It is important to check your knowledge using the following Multiple Choice Questions.

Multiple Choice Questions

Question 1

Simon, an actor, had contracted with a theatre company to hire their premises to perform a play. The play was unsuccessful, and Simon did not make enough money to pay the hire fee when it became due. Simon eventually agreed that he would pay the fee in instalments over a period of nine months. The theatre company agreed to accept a reduced amount for the first six months and an increased amount for the following three months to make up the difference. Simon has now disputed paying the outstanding increased amount for the last three months as he believes he has paid enough in full consideration of the debt.

Which of the following best describes the legal position?

A. Simon's promise to pay part of a debt in the discharge of the whole debt is not good consideration for a promise to accept less. The theatre cannot demand the full amount.
B. Simon's promise to pay part of a debt in the discharge of the whole debt is good consideration for a promise to accept less. The theatre cannot demand the full amount.
C. Simon's promise to pay part of a debt in the discharge of the whole debt is not good consideration for a promise to accept less. The theatre can demand the full amount.
D. The theatre company can rely on promissory estoppel to sue Simon.
E. Simon has only provided sufficient consideration, not adequate consideration, and therefore the promise to pay less is not contractually binding.

Question 2

Elise has agreed with Charlotte to distribute leaflets for her new gym opening this year in Bush Central, her local area. Elise has agreed on a fee of £200 to distribute 200 leaflets for Charlotte over a period of three days. Elise goes back to Charlotte after a day and tells her that she has finished distributing half the leaflets. Charlotte is so impressed that she pays Elise the £200 straight away and offers her a fee of £80 to distribute 80 more leaflets, as she realised that she meant to give Charlotte 280 leaflets initially. Charlotte instructs Elise to deliver the extra 80 leaflets to a particular area to attract wealthy potential clients. Once Elise has finished, she goes back to Charlotte to ask for her extra £80.

Which of the following best describes the legal position?

A. There is an existing contract for leaflet distribution for a fee of £200 between Charlotte and Elise. As the initial contract is for 200 leaflets, Elise has gone over and beyond her pre-existing contractual duty by delivering the extra 80 leaflets. Charlotte is legally obliged to pay the extra £80 to Elise.

B. There is an existing contract for leaflet distribution for a fee of £200 between Charlotte and Elise. As the initial contract is for 200 leaflets, which should have included the extra 80 leaflets, Elise has not gone over and beyond her pre-existing contractual duty by delivering the extra 80 leaflets. Charlotte is not obliged to pay the extra £80 to Elise.

C. The agreement between Charlotte and Elise amounts to past consideration, which is therefore not good consideration. Charlotte will not be legally obliged to pay Elise the extra £80.

D. There is a lack of consideration from both parties and therefore, only the initial amount of £200 will be enforceable.

E. The agreement between Charlotte and Elise amounts to past consideration, which is therefore good consideration. Charlotte will be legally obliged to pay Elise the extra £80.

Question 3

Daniel has just graduated from university. Daniel has no experience in law and would like to work as a legal assistant. He has been advised to write a student article for a leading student law journal. Daniel approaches the editor of the journal and offers to write an article on his experience as a first-generation student in a London-based university, to which the editor agrees. Daniel agrees to write the article without payment. However, the editor is so impressed with the article that he publishes it and offers to pay Daniel £750. Daniel has approached the editor for payment. The editor is now refusing to pay the £750.

Which of the following best describes the legal position?

A. Daniel will be able to enforce the promise of £750, as he has provided consideration.
B. Daniel will not be able to enforce the promise, as it is an executory consideration.
C. Daniel will not be able to enforce the promise because of past consideration.
D. Daniel will be able to enforce the promise because there is an implied promise that payment will be made.
E. Daniel will be able to enforce the promise as it is executed consideration.

4 Privity of contract and rights of third parties

4.1 Chapter overview

This chapter considers the principle of privity of contract. The chapter begins by explaining the basic rule of privity, which is that only the parties to a contract may sue or be sued upon it. There are, however, a number of exceptions where third parties may be able to enforce rights contained in a contract. These exceptions are identified and discussed in this chapter, beginning with the rights given to third parties to enforce terms of a contract by the Contracts (Rights of Third Parties) Act 1999 and then proceeding to more limited or specific exceptions.

4.2 The rule of privity

The basic principle of privity is a simple one. Only the parties to a contract may enforce it, and the contract may only be enforced against the parties to it.[1] We have seen in Chapters 1–3 that contract law will only create and enforce legal obligations when certain requirements are met, chiefly that the parties are in agreement (with a valid offer and acceptance), that both parties have provided good consideration, and that the contract has been made with the intention to create legal relations. Given these strict requirements, it is logical that the law will not allow those who have not been part of the agreement and have not provided their own consideration to either enforce contractual rights, or to be liable under the contract. This links back to the principle covered in Chapter 3 that *consideration must move from the promisee.*

4.3 Exceptions to the rule

Consider the following two scenarios:

Scenario 1

A mother decides to buy her daughter a second-hand car worth £2,000 *as a gift for her 21st birthday. Under the terms of the contract, the car is specified to have a*

1 *Dunlop Pneumatic Tyre Co Ltd v Selfridge & Co Ltd* [1915] AC 847.

DOI: 10.4324/9781032642161-6

mileage of 20,000 miles, but it later transpires that the car has actually travelled 125,000 miles, making it much less valuable.

Scenario 2

A business owner decides to retire and agrees to sell his business to a new buyer. As part of the agreement, the buyer promises to pay the business owner 20% of the profits from the business for the next 10 years, but it is specified that if the seller dies, the payments will instead be made to the seller's wife. The seller dies two years into the agreement, and the buyer fails to make the promised payments to his wife.

In both situations, it would be impossible for either contract to be successfully enforced. The rule of privity would prevent either the daughter in the first scenario or the wife in the second scenario from successfully claiming, because they are both third parties to these contracts. The person who could claim would be the mother and the husband (or rather his estate), respectively. The problem is that neither of these parties has suffered any loss. The mother does not have any legal interest in the car, so the decrease in value cannot be considered her loss. Similarly, the husband has not failed to receive any money due to him. The first scenario is set out in Figure 4.1 – notice how there is no consideration coming from the daughter.

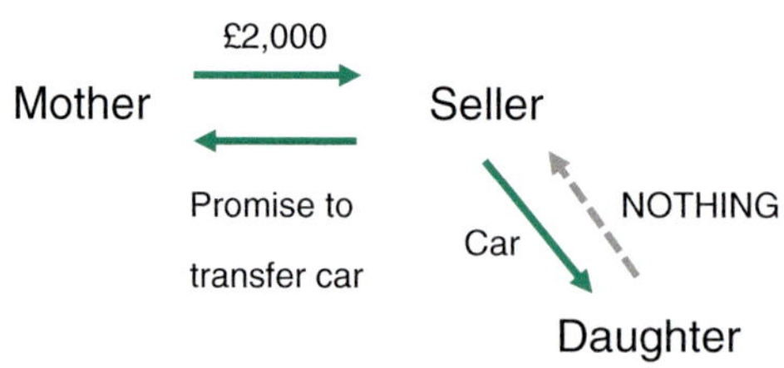

Figure 4.1 Privity in practice

Due to these problems, a wide range of exceptions have developed over time in order to try to circumvent the rule of privity. These exceptions vary widely, coming from many different areas of law. Some were created by common law, while others are statutory. However, one key element all of these exceptions have in common is that they all relate to allowing a third party to enforce the contract, rather than allowing a contract to be enforced against someone who never agreed to the contractual obligations.

4.4 The Contracts (Rights of Third Parties) Act 1999

The widest exception to the general rule of privity is the Contracts (Rights of Third Parties) Act 1999 ("the 1999 Act"). This Act was passed specifically to allow third parties to enforce contracts in certain situations. The Act will by default apply to all contracts made after 11 May 2000, but as we will see, the parties to a contract may choose to exclude the Act from applying. Where the Act is not excluded, it allows a person who is not a party to a contract to enforce a term of that contract if one of two conditions applies:[2]

1. The contract expressly provides that the third party may enforce it;
2. The term the third party wishes to enforce purports to confer a benefit on the third party.

We will look at both conditions in turn.

4.4.1 Contract expressly provides for enforcement

Where the contract expressly provides that a third party may enforce a term, that third party may do so under the 1999 Act.[3] This is a very straightforward method of guaranteeing that a third party can enforce the term, but it does require the parties to agree in advance that the third party will have the right to do so, and for them to expressly state this within the contractual terms.

4.4.2 Term confers benefit on third party

As an alternative, a third party may also enforce a term where that particular term purports to confer a benefit on him or her.[4] Therefore to rely on this condition, the third party must be able to show that the term was intended by the contracting parties to confer a benefit on the third party. The right does not apply if on a "proper construction" of the contract it appears the parties did not intend the term to be enforceable by the third party.[5] The presumption is that the parties did intend the term to be enforceable, so the defendant must prove that this was not the case.

Therefore, just because a term incidentally benefits a third party, that term is not necessarily enforceable by that third party. Consider the following scenario:

> Talcum Transport is a logistics firm that has successfully completed a number of contracts with Urban Undergarments, a clothing company. Urban Undergarments owe Talcum Transport nearly £200,000 in outstanding payments under these contracts, but are undergoing a cash flow crisis and may go out of business. The directors of Talcum Transport learn that Urban Undergarments are owed £400,000 by Vivid Vests, a clothes retailer that has been selling

2 S1 Contracts (Rights of Third Parties) Act 1999.
3 S1(1)(a) Contracts (Rights of Third Parties) Act 1999.
4 S1(1)(b) Contracts (Rights of Third Parties) Act 1999.
5 S1(2) Contracts (Rights of Third Parties) Act 1999.

Urban Undergarments products. Can Talcum Transport enforce the contract between Urban Undergarments and Vivid Vests?

Even though enforcing the contract would benefit Talcum Transport, because presumably some of the money paid to Urban Undergarments could in turn be used to settle the debt to Talcum Transport, it is very unlikely that they can enforce the contract using the 1999 Act. The term, which requires payment of money to Urban Undergarments, does not purport to confer a benefit on Talcum Transport. The term was not agreed by the parties with the intention of benefitting Talcum Transport.

Even where the term does purport to confer a benefit on the claimant third party, the right to enforce the term will be subject to the contract as a whole.[6] Thus if another term limits that right (for example, setting a time limit from the breach by which the claim must be brought) it will take effect.

4.4.3 Requirement third party is identified

Whether a claim is based on the contract providing for third-party enforcement or on the term conferring a benefit on the third party, the third party must also show that they are expressly identified in the contract.[7] The third party can be identified by name, or as a member of a class, or as answering a particular description. Importantly, the third party does not need to be in existence at the time the contract is made.

4.4.4 Express term excluding the 1999 Act

It is perfectly permissible for the parties to the initial contract to exclude the 1999 Act from applying to the contract, by including an express clause to the effect that third parties will have no rights to enforce any term of the contract under the 1999 Act.

4.4.5 Summary of the effect of the 1999 Act

Figure 4.2 explains the operation of the 1999 Act.

4.5 Other methods of enforcing third-party rights

The 1999 Act is an important method of enforcing third-party rights, but as explained in the preceding sections, it does not provide an effective mechanism in

6 S1(4) Contracts (Rights of Third Parties) Act 1999.
7 S1(3) Contracts (Rights of Third Parties) Act 1999.

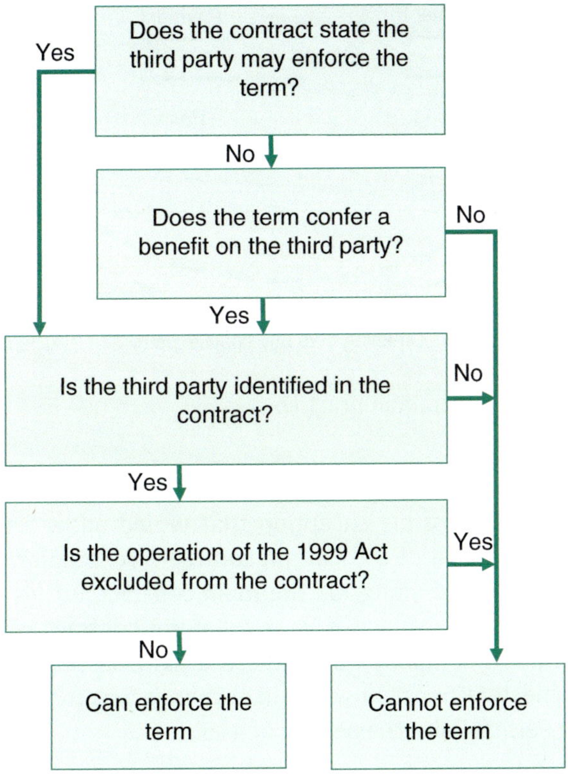

Figure 4.2 Applying the Contracts (Rights of Third Parties) Act 1999

all cases. As such, various other exceptions, most of which developed prior to the Act coming into force, remain relevant in certain situations.

4.5.1 Collateral contracts

Consider the following scenario:

> Northchester Council contract with Oliver, a professional painter, to paint the famous Northchester Pier. The Council tell Oliver that they have been told by Perfect Paint that their special weatherproof paint is guaranteed for 10 years and that Oliver should use this paint for the job. Oliver buys the paint and paints the pier, but the paint is defective and soon begins to flake off.

Applying the basic principle of privity, Northchester Council do not seem to have a contractual remedy. They are not in a contractual relationship with Perfect Paint themselves. They cannot sue on Oliver's contract to buy the paint, because they are not a party to it. They are unlikely to be expressly identified in the contract, which would preclude a claim under the 1999 Act. Oliver could sue for breach of contract, but Oliver has not lost anything financially – he has been paid to paint

Figure 4.3 A collateral contract in practice

the pier and he does not lose anything by the fact the paint is now flaking off. In these circumstances, a possible exception that would allow the Council to sue Oliver comes from the idea of a collateral contract.[8] A "collateral" contract is an additional contract, created alongside the main contract. In this case, it could be argued that Northchester Council have a collateral contract with Perfect Paint, under which the paint company guarantee the paint lasting 10 years. The consideration Northchester Council provided in exchange was to tell Oliver to use that paint – i.e. giving Perfect Paint the benefit of a sale.

Figure 4.3 shows the way a collateral contract can operate to avoid the privity problem.

4.5.2 Claims for specific performance

Another method of enforcing a term which benefits a third party is through one party to the contract bringing an action against the other, not for damages but for the remedy of specific performance. This remedy is considered in more detail in Chapter 18, but it has the effect of requiring a party to do something which they promised to do under the contract.

Consider the following scenario:

> Alex agrees with Beryl to buy Beryl's business. As part of the agreement, Alex agrees to pay Beryl £100,000 up front, and to then make an annual payment of £20,000 to Beryl each year for the next 10 years. The parties agree that in the event Beryl dies within that period, Alex will instead pay £20,000 to Beryl's partner Cinzia. Beryl dies two years later but Alex fails to pay Cinzia as promised. Cinzia is the executor of Beryl's estate. Is there anything Cinzia can do to enforce the contract?

8 See *Shanklin Pier v Detel Products* [1951] 2 KB 854 on which this example is based.

While Cinzia has no personal right against Alex, not being party to the contract with him, as executor of the estate she can claim in Beryl's name against Alex for breach of contract. Beryl, or rather her estate, has not lost anything financially (because Alex is now due to pay Cinzia, not Beryl's estate) so damages are of no use, but a claim in Beryl's name for specific performance would mean the court ordering Alex to pay Cinzia as agreed in the contract.[9]

As you will learn in Chapter 18, the downside of specific performance is that it can only be claimed in very specific or limited circumstances, where damages are not an adequate remedy. The other issue is that outside of the very specific circumstances of Cinzia, who was administering Beryl's estate, normally the third party will have to persuade the other party to the contract to bring the claim (potentially at considerable cost) for specific performance.

4.5.3 Contracts for enjoyment and entertainment

There is a very specific line of cases which began based on claims by holidaymakers against tour operators who had failed, in breach of contract, to provide a sufficient standard of holiday. Under this line of cases, it was established that not only could a holidaymaker claim damages for their own distress and disappointment in such situations, but that they could also claim a sum on behalf of the other people they went on holiday with.[10] This exception only applies in very specific circumstances:

- The contract must be one made for entertainment and enjoyment, as otherwise damages for distress and disappointment are not recoverable;
- To claim such damages on behalf of others, there must be evidence that one party contracted on behalf of a group for reasons of convenience.[11]

4.5.4 Assignment and agency

Assignment refers to a legal transfer of the benefit of a contractual right from one person (the assignor) to another (the assignee). A common example of assignment in practice is where a party owed money under a contract "sells" the debt, at a lower price, to a specialist debt collector. They assign the right to be paid under the contract, and the debt collector can then enforce that right directly against the debtor.

Agency refers to where one person (the agent) is given the authority to enter into a contract on behalf of another (the principal). In such a situation, the principal can sue on the contract (and be sued on the contract, unlike in most other exceptions) despite the fact that the actual agreement was between the other party and the agent.

9 See *Beswick v Beswick* [1968] AC 58.
10 *Jackson v Horizon Holidays Ltd* [1975] 1 WLR 1468.
11 *Woodar Investment Development Ltd v Wimpey Construction (UK) Ltd* [1980] 1 WLR 277.

Therefore, agency is something which must be established before the contract is made, while assignment is something which takes place after the contract has been made.

4.5.5 Relying on exemption clauses

This is a complex area of law which developed in regards to the complicated commercial arrangements used in the shipping industry, where such clauses exempting a third party's liability have become known as "Himalaya clauses". Such clauses grant protection from liability to other persons (often employees or independent contractors) and will be effective if:[12]

1. The clause clearly states the third party is to be protected;
2. The clause makes it clear that the party is contracting as an agent for the third party;
3. The contracting party has authority to contract for the third party (which can be implied based on commercial good sense)[13];
4. The third party provided some form of consideration (which may be what they promised to do for the contracting party).[14]

4.5.6 Claims using other areas of law

In some cases, rather than seeking to rely on exceptions, the simplest solution may be to bring a claim for an alternative cause of action. The most notable alternative in many cases is a claim in the *tort of negligence*. For example, a consumer is injured by a defective product sold to them by a shop. The defect is not the fault of the shop, but rather the manufacturer. While the consumer has no contractual relationship with the manufacturer, it is well established that the manufacturer of a product owes a duty of care to its end user in the tort of negligence.[15]

Another area of law that can assist is *trusts law*. Where party A makes a promise as part of a contract with party B to provide a benefit to a third party, C, C can argue that B holds the right to enforce the contract on trust for C's benefit. As the beneficiary of this trust, C then has the right to the substance of the trust, which is in turn the right to enforce the contract. This exception does require evidence of intention to create the trust, not just intention to benefit the third party, which can be difficult to provide.

12 The four requirements were first set out by Lord Reid in *Scruttons Ltd v Midland Silicones Ltd* [1962] AC 446.

13 *Owners of the Ship "Borvigilant" v Owners of the "Romina C"* [2003] EWCA Civ 935.

14 *New Zealand Shipping Co Ltd v A.M. Satterthwaite & Co Ltd (The Eurymedon)* [1975] AC 154.

15 As famously established in *Donoghue v Stevenson* [1932] AC 562.

4.6 Enforcing obligations against a third party

All of the discussion above has been about when a third party can enforce a contract against one of the parties to it – i.e. sue on the contract. The law is much less willing to allow for the converse situation, of a contractual party enforcing obligations against a third party. This is not provided for under the 1999 Act. There are very few situations in which a third party can be sued on a contract, but one example is the mechanism of restrictive covenants in land law – in some circumstances, a covenant restricting the owner's use of their land made by a previous owner can be enforced against a subsequent owner.

Chapter 4 Revision Points

Third parties to the contract

- Rule of privity – cannot sue or be sued
- Contracts (Rights of Third Parties) Act 1999
  - Can enforce if contract expressly says so
  - Or if term for benefit of third party *and* not inconsistent with contract
  - Third party must be identified in contract
  - Can exclude Act from applying
- Other ways around rule
  - Collateral contract
  - Specific performance
  - Damages for a group (enjoyment/entertainment)
  - Assignment
  - Agency
  - "Himalaya clauses" excluding liability
  - Tort
  - Trust

It is important to check your knowledge using the following Multiple Choice Questions.

Multiple Choice Questions

Question 1

A husband purchased a luxury spa experience for his wife, which included a hot stone massage treatment and access to the sauna complex. The contract between the husband and the spa company stated that the spa experience was for the benefit of the wife. When his wife visited the spa, she was told there were no massage therapists available so she could not receive the treatment, and that the sauna complex was closed.

Can the contract be enforced against the spa?

A. Yes, by the wife because the contract expressly provides that she may enforce it and she is identified in the contract.
B. Yes, by the wife because the contract includes terms for her benefit and she is identified in the contract.
C. Yes, by the husband because he has suffered loss as a result of the breach of contract.
D. No, because there is a collateral contract between the husband and his wife.
E. No, because the rule of privity prevents the wife from enforcing a contract she is a third party to.

Question 2

A gardener agrees with a homeowner to carry out landscaping work on the back garden of the home. Halfway through the project, the homeowner dies. The gardener takes on another project and refuses to return to finish the landscaping work. The homeowner's daughter, who is also the executor of the homeowner's estate, wishes to enforce the contract.

What advice should be given to the daughter?

A. She can enforce the contract in her own name, because she will inherit the home and the contract is thus for her benefit.
B. She can enforce the contract in her own name, because she is acting as an agent of her father the homeowner.
C. She cannot enforce the contract in her own name, but she may be able to seek specific performance in her capacity as executor.
D. She cannot enforce the contract in either her own name or the name of the homeowner, due to the rule of privity.
E. She can claim damages on the basis that this was contract for enjoyment, pleasure, and entertainment.

PART 2

Contents of a contract

5 Express terms and incorporation of terms

5.1 Chapter overview

Part 1 of this book has considered the various legal issues relating to formation of a contract. In Part 2, you will go on to learn about the contents of the contract. Contracts are made up of terms (terms are sometimes also referred to as "clauses"). This chapter will consider express terms, terms outwardly expressed by the parties. When establishing what the express terms of a particular contract are, the first question is to establish which statements made by the parties have the status of a term, and which are mere representations. After considering the law on terms and representations, the chapter goes on to consider particular issues that affect contracts made partly in writing. Finally, the chapter examines the different methods by which express terms can be incorporated into a contract.

5.2 Terms and representations

A contract is made up of terms. Any breach of a term allows for a claim for breach of contract, and in some circumstances for the "innocent" (non-breaching) party to escape from the contract entirely. It is therefore very important to be able to establish exactly what the terms of the contract are. In the course of making a contract, it is very common that plenty of statements will have been made by one or both parties, not all of which will have the force of contractual terms. The law distinguishes between three types of statement, which might occur in pre-contractual discussions, as shown in Figure 5.1.

Puffs are statements simply made as part of "sales talk". An example would be an advertising slogan promising that a product will "make you feel great" – it is not intended to be taken literally.

While discounting "mere puffs" can be a matter of common sense, it can be more difficult to determine whether a particular statement is a term or a representation. The distinction is important, because breach of a term allows for the full range of remedies discussed in Chapters 16–18, and in some cases for the innocent party to terminate the contract (see Chapter 14). A representation can only allow for a claim in misrepresentation, which is covered in Chapter 9.

DOI: 10.4324/9781032642161-8

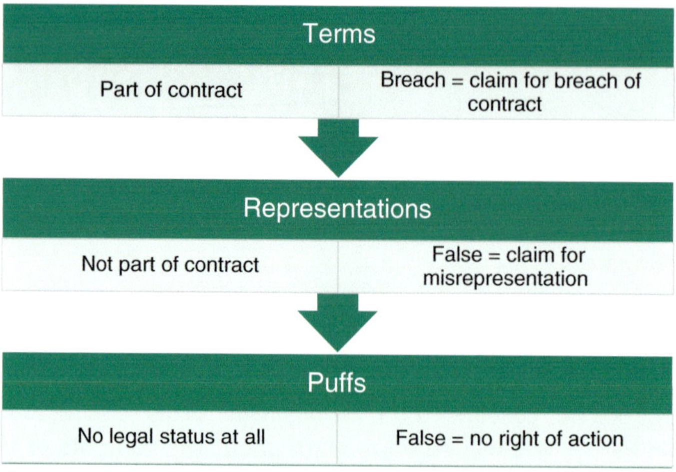

Figure 5.1 Distinguishing terms, representations, and puffs

5.2.1 An objective approach

The court will determine whether a statement is a term or a representation by looking at the intention of the parties – did the parties intend for the statement to give rise to contractual liability?[1] They will take an objective approach to deciding intention. This means that rather than looking subjectively at whether a party might have personally believed a statement to be a term (or a representation), the court will look at the external evidence to determine what the parties intended. Over time, the way the courts have done this has created a set of secondary tests or principles. None of these "tests" is determinative, and they can contradict one another in a particular case, but they are a useful guide to factors the court will consider when determining intention. When considering these principles in the following sections, keep in mind the following scenario:

> Rhys posts on social media that he has a television for sale. Stefanie is interested and visits Rhys to inspect the TV. Rhys tells Stefanie that the TV is a 2022 model with three HDMI ports. Stefanie asks Rhys if the TV can play 8K video, because she is not interested if it cannot. Rhys assures Stefanie that it can. Rhys allows Stefanie to examine the TV for herself. Two weeks later, Stefanie calls Rhys and asks whether the price includes delivery to her house. Rhys says yes and Stefanie agrees to buy the television for £1,000. Stefanie has now learned that the TV is a 2021 model, with two HDMI ports. It cannot play 8K video, and Rhys has told Stefanie she must collect the TV herself.

1 *Heilbut Symons and Co. v Buckleton* [1913] AC 30.

5.2.2 The importance attached test

The more important it was for one party that a statement made by the other was true, the more likely the statement will be incorporated as a term of the contract rather than merely a representation. This is most apparent when the statement is so important, the other party would not have made the contract if it was not truly the case.[2]

In the scenario above, Stefanie tells Rhys that it is essential that the TV has 8K video. It is likely that this is a term of the contract, because without this statement, there would have been no agreement. As such, this is a fundamental part of the contract, and it is highly likely that this statement will be incorporated into the contract as a term.

5.2.3 Special knowledge of parties

The court will consider any special knowledge on behalf of one or other party about the subject of the statement. The court is less concerned with exactly how expert one or the other party is, and more concerned with the relative knowledge between the parties – which party is in a better position to determine the truth of the statement?[3]

In Stefanie's scenario, imagine that Stefanie is an electronics trader, an expert in different makes and models of television. In that instance, she is probably in at least as good a position as Rhys to determine if the TV is a 2021 or 2022 model, and that statement would be more likely to be a representation as a result.

On the contrary, if Stefanie has no expertise in TVs, the position may be different. Rhys, who bought the TV initially and probably has an order confirmation or receipt, might be in a better position to know the truth. In that instance, the statement may constitute a term.

5.2.4 Independent verification

In a similar way to looking at which party has the greater knowledge to determine the truth of the statement, the court may also look at how much opportunity the party to whom the statement was made had to check or verify the truth for themselves.[4] Where a party assures the other that they guarantee the truth of the statement and there is no need to check it, that is more likely to be a term. However, in a situation like that of Stefanie and Rhys, where a party is encouraged to inspect goods, it may be that a statement like the number of HDMI ports is merely a representation. This may in turn amount to a separate claim for misrepresentation (discussed further in Chapter 9).

2 See for example *Bannerman v White* (1861) 10 CB NS 844.
3 See for example *Esso Petroleum Co v Mardon* [1976] QB 801.
4 See for example *Schawel v Reade* [1913] 2 IR 81.

5.2.5 Timing of statement

The closer in time a statement is to the making of the contract, the more likely it is to be part of that contract (and thus a term) rather than merely part of the background negotiations (and thus a representation).[5] Consider Stefanie's query about delivery – she asks this right before deciding to enter into the contract. This overlaps with the idea of importance, as clearly statements made close to the time of contracting will be uppermost in a party's mind.

5.2.6 Reduction of statement into writing

Where a contract is made partly in writing and partly orally, the decision to include a statement within the written contract is likely to suggest that it is a term. There is a link here to the idea of importance – if the parties have written down some statements (but not others), it is likely that those were the most fundamental statements about what was agreed.

5.3 Written contracts

In general, there is no requirement that a contract must be made in writing.[6] However, for clarity and for evidential reasons, it is common for parties to place some or all of their contract into a written document. Problems can arise when one party claims that the written contract does not reflect the entire agreement, or can only be interpreted by reference to other evidence.[7]

5.3.1 The parol evidence rule

The traditional approach to written contracts is that the written document comprises the whole of the contract, and so a party cannot adduce extrinsic evidence to contradict, vary, add to, or subtract from the terms of the written contract. This is known as the "parol evidence" rule. It applies to any evidence outside of the written contractual document – this might be things said, things done, or other written documents. However, the rule is subject to two crucial limitations.

- It only applies to situations where the contract is wholly written – so it does not apply where the evidence shows *the document was not intended to express the entire agreement*, such as in partly written and partly oral contracts.
- Even in a wholly written contract, a *collateral contract* can be found running alongside the main contract which contains additional terms. A collateral contract is a second, separate contract between the parties. Therefore it would be binding in its own right – rather than being (parol) evidence of additional terms in the first contract.

5 See for example *Routledge v McKay* [1954] 1 WLR 615.

6 Although there are some exceptions, notably contracts for the creation or disposal of an interest in land, S53 Law of Property Act 1925.

7 *Bank of Australasia v Palmer* [1897] AC 540.

The effect of these two exceptions is to make the parol evidence rule of limited value. A party can always argue that extrinsic evidence is required either because it is part of the contract (i.e. the document was not intended to express the entire agreement) or because it formed a second, collateral contract. To try to avoid this, drafters have created clauses that seek to prevent this.

5.3.2 Entire agreement clauses

An entire agreement clause is one which states the written document in which it is contained is the "entire agreement" between the parties. As such, it tries to prevent a party from stating that the contract is actually made up of a number of documents, or is partly written and partly oral. Entire agreement clauses will be upheld by the courts as long as they have been validly incorporated into the contract. They will still need to be interpreted in the same way as any other contractual term – so a poorly drafted entire agreement clause might, for example, prevent the other party from relying on extrinsic evidence of additional terms, but might not preclude a claim in misrepresentation based on these extrinsic statements being false.

5.3.3 No oral modification clauses

A similar but distinct clause is a no oral modification clause (sometimes abbreviated to a "NOM clause"). This clause also seeks to prevent a party relying on external evidence to alter the contract, but the difference is that a NOM clause refers to extrinsic discussions after the contract has been made. A NOM clause will state that neither party may vary the terms of the initial contract unless that variation is in writing – so, for example, a telephone conversation about the contract would not be sufficient to vary it.

5.4 Incorporation of terms

The preceding sections have considered what statements made by parties to the contract may be permitted to constitute terms. However, in order for a statement to actually take effect as an express term of the contract, it must as a matter of fact have been incorporated into that contract. The law recognises three distinct methods of incorporation: signature, reasonable notice, and a consistent course of dealing.

5.4.1 Incorporation by signature

The most straightforward method of incorporation applies to where the agreement is reduced to writing and this document is signed by one or more parties. Any party who signs a contractual document will, as a general rule, be bound by the terms contained within it. It is important to specify that the document must be contractual – so signing a purely administrative document like a receipt which simply records payment may not bind a party to the terms.

Signature traditionally meant physical signature on a paper document, but electronic signatures also constitute a valid signature.[8] This can include a wide range of electronic communications, including putting one's name at the bottom of an email, ticking a box to accept terms and conditions, or clicking a button on a website.

Crucially, it does not matter if the party has actually read the document they have signed, or whether if they have read it, they have understood it. The only circumstances in which a signature will not bind a party will be where a vitiating factor is present, such as misrepresentation, duress, or undue influence. For more information on vitiating elements, see Chapters 9–12 of this book.

5.4.2 Incorporation by reasonable notice

If a party has not signed a document containing a particular term, the term will still be incorporated into the contract if that party had reasonable notice of it. This is particularly relevant where terms are included in a separate document, or in a physical contractual notice. In daily life, this often relates to exclusion clauses, for example a notice in a car park stating that the operator is not liable for any loss or damage to belongings left in vehicles.

In order to constitute reasonable notice, the notice must be:

1 Provided at or before the time of contracting;
2 Contained in a contractual document;
3 Reasonable in its extent.

Notice at the time of contracting

Because a contract is formed at the moment of agreement (see Chapter 1), any terms that one party purports to include after acceptance will not be a valid part of the contract. For example:

> Sadhya visits a local swimming pool. She pays at the pool entrance, including a £5 payment to use a secure storage locker. When she puts her belongings in the locker, she sees a notice on the inside of the locker door stating the swimming pool operator is not liable for any loss or damage. Her belongings are stolen from the locker, which had a defective lock.

In this example, Sadhya made a contract at the entrance – so the notice came too late to incorporate the term into the contract, and therefore is ineffective. The term is not incorporated.

8 S7 Electronic Communications Act 2000.

Notice in a contractual document

The means by which the notice is provided is also relevant. The document in which the notice is contained must be one which a reasonable person could expect to contain conditions. For example:

> Uzman visits a luxury hotel. On arrival at the hotel, a valet is waiting to park Uzman's car for him. When Uzman gives the valet his car keys, the valet gives him a slip of paper with a code on it, which Uzman can use to get his car back at the end of his stay. Unbeknownst to Uzman, on the back of this paper is a term excluding liability for damage to the car while it is on the hotel premises.

The reasonable person would assume that the piece of paper was a practical token used to identify which car should be returned to Uzman – not a contractual document containing important terms. As such, it is unlikely that the term will take effect.

Incorporation by reference is possible – so a document provided might state that the full terms and conditions are available elsewhere.

Extent of notice must be reasonable

This is a question of fact in each case. What is sufficient notice will be very dependent on the specific circumstances and can also change with time – for example, today it is quite common for a contract to refer to terms and conditions which are available on a website. The question is not whether the party actually knew of the term(s) in question, but whether enough was done by the party seeking to rely on the term (often to limit or exclude liability) to bring the existence of the term to the attention of the other party.

It is clear that the more onerous (burdensome or troublesome) the term, the greater the degree of notice required.[9] This is sometimes referred to as the "red hand rule", because one way of making a particularly onerous term stand out in a document would be to include a drawing of a red hand pointing to the term. This is just an example, and other common ways of drawing attention to a term include placing it in a larger font, in bold text, or in a separate box; or to make the other party aware of its existence by providing separate notice, such as in a "key terms" document included with the full contract. Today, it is very common to ask a party to expressly note they have been made aware of the terms of the contract – for example, in a contract made via a website or app, the user will often need to check a box stating they are aware of the terms and conditions before they can accept the contract.

9 *Interfoto Picture Library Ltd v Stiletto Visual Programmes Ltd* [1988] QB 433.

5.4.3 Incorporation by consistent course of dealing

One further method of incorporation is through a consistent prior course of dealing between the parties. Where the parties have consistently incorporated a term (through signature or reasonable notice) in their past dealings, it is possible that it will be incorporated on a later occasion where these other methods are not used. This requires a consistent course of dealing on the same standard terms – what is consistent will be a matter of fact for the court to decide in each case. For example:

> Eberechi takes his car once a month to Florence's car wash. He has done this every month for five years. Every month, Florence gives Eberechi a "disclaimer notice" which she asks Eberechi to sign. The notice includes a term excluding liability for any damage to the paintwork on Eberechi's car caused by the operation of the car wash. One month Florence forgets to give Eberechi the paper to sign.

It is likely that on this occasion, the term will be incorporated, because it has been consistently included in all previous agreements, and this course of dealing has been frequent (once a month) and consistent (every month for five years).

5.5 Categorisation of terms

Once the court has established which statements will make up the terms of the contract, it also must decide for each term which category the term falls into (this also applies to implied terms, discussed further in the next chapter, Chapter 6). Terms can be categorised as being of one of three types:

1 Conditions;
2 Warranties;
3 Innominate.

The reason it is important to categorise terms is that different remedies will be available on breach of a term, depending on which category it falls into. Breach of contract is considered further in Chapters 14 and 15, and the remedies in the event of breach are discussed in Chapters 16–18.

5.5.1 Conditions

Conditions are considered fundamental terms which go to the root of the contract.[10] For example, in an employment contract, terms which are conditions would include the availability of the employee to work during their working hours, and payment of wages by the employer.

10 *Graves v Legg* (1854) 9 Ex 709.

Breach of a condition will always allow the other party to terminate the contract, as well as claiming damages. Breach of a condition does not automatically end the contract, however – whether the contract ends is at the choice of the non-breaching party (see Chapter 15 for more on this point).

5.5.2 Warranties

Warranties are terms of the contract which are less important, or are collateral to the main purpose of the contract. For example, in a contract to purchase a television, the inclusion of fittings to allow the television to be fixed to the wall might be a warranty. Breach of a warranty allows a claim for damages, but does not allow the non-breaching party to terminate the contract.

5.5.3 Innominate terms

Traditionally contract law only recognised conditions and warranties, but in modern contract law the courts also recognise the existence of "innominate" terms (sometimes also called "intermediate" terms). An innominate term is a term which is neither a condition nor a warranty. Instead, it is a term where the parties must "wait and see" what the effect of breach will be. A term is likely to be considered innominate when it could be breached in different ways; so breach could lead to relatively minor consequences or to much more serious consequences.[11]

When an innominate term is breached, the court will consider whether the effect of the breach was to deprive the non-breaching party of substantially the whole benefit they were to obtain from the contract. If it does deprive them of substantially the whole benefit, they will be entitled to terminate the contract as well as claiming damages. If not, they may only claim damages, but not terminate the contract.

It is important to remember that the term itself remains innominate – the court does not use the consequences of breach to decide if the term is a condition or a warranty, it uses the consequences of breach to decide what remedy will be granted for breach of the innominate term.

5.5.4 Terminology of the parties

It should be noted that the parties may describe a term as a "condition" or a "warranty" in the text of their agreement. The court will take heed of the parties' labels, but this will not always be determinative or conclusive – if the court does not believe that the true intention of the parties was to classify a term in this way, it can depart from the label used by the parties.[12]

11 *Hongkong Fir Shipping Co Ltd v Kawasaki Kisen Kaisha Ltd* [1962] 2 QB 26.
12 *L. G. Schuler A. G. v Wickman Machine Tool Sales Ltd* [1974] AC 235.

It is also true that in everyday language, the words "condition" and "warranty" can have different meanings. In particular, there is a tendency to call a contract as a whole "terms and conditions" and a tendency in consumer contracts to consider a "warranty" to mean a specific agreement under which a seller or manufacturer promises to repair or replace an item during a particular time period after sale. These uses of the words condition and warranty should be distinguished from the legal sense in which they are used to categorise terms as explained above.

5.5.5 Time of the essence

It is a settled principle of common law that terms which make "time of the essence", i.e. which set a strict deadline for performance, will usually be classified as conditions.[13] Where there is no time stipulated in a contract, both parties must perform their contractual obligations within a reasonable time. However, where "time is of the essence" (in other words, where time is stipulated in the contract to be an important contractual obligation), the obligation must be carried out within that time, otherwise one party may repudiate the contract and receive just damages. In some cases, the circumstances, subject matter, or context may make it obvious that "time is of the essence", such as a delivery of perishable goods by a certain date for a dinner party or wedding reception. See Figure 5.2.

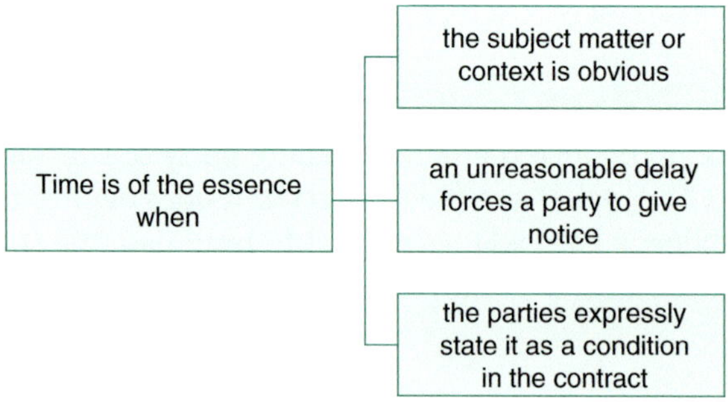

Figure 5.2 Time of the essence clauses

13 See discussion in *Lombard North Central Plc v Butterworth* [1987] QB 527.

Chapter 5 Revision Points

Terms and representations

- Test is objective
- What was the intention of the parties?
- Look at:
    - Importance attached
    - Special knowledge
    - Independent verification
    - Timing
    - Reduced into writing

Written contracts

- Parol evidence rule
    - Exception: partly written partly oral
    - Exception: collateral contract
- Limit by drafting
    - Entire agreement clauses
    - No oral modification clauses

Incorporation

- Signature
    - Irrelevant if read
    - Exception: vitiating factors
- Reasonable notice
    - Timing
    - Contractual document
    - Extent of notice
- Consistent course of dealings

It is important to check your knowledge using the following Multiple Choice Questions.

Multiple Choice Questions

Question 1

A pet food company is purchasing hay from a farmer for use in rabbit food. During negotiations, the company asks the farmer whether certain pesticides have been used on the hay. The company makes clear that because its food is advertised as "pesticide-free" it has no interest in buying the hay if pesticides have been used. The farmer assures them they have not. A week later the company agree to purchase the hay. A few weeks later, when the hay arrives at the pet food factory, it becomes clear that it has been treated with pesticides.

Which statement correctly explains whether the non-use of pesticides was a term of the contract?

A. The statement is not a term, because the pet food company could have independently verified whether the hay had been treated with pesticides.
B. The statement is a "mere puff", because it was said as part of the farmer's sales pitch and was not intended to be taken seriously.
C. The statement is a term, because the pet food company has specialist knowledge of pet products.
D. The statement is not a term, because there was a week's delay between the statement being made and the contract being formed.
E. The statement is a term, because of the importance attached to the statement.

Question 2

A holidaymaker visits a theme park. She has visited the park once before, two years previously. At the entrance to the park, the visitor purchases a ticket which gives her the right to enter the park and to ride on the large rollercoaster inside the park. Once inside the park, the visitor queues to ride the rollercoaster. While in the queue, she notices a sign with large red text stating that the park is not liable for any damage to personal property caused when riding the rollercoaster. While riding the rollercoaster, her expensive designer watch is scratched by the machinery.

Will the exclusion clause be incorporated into the visitor's contract with the theme park?

A. Yes, because her previous visit to the park establishes a consistent course of dealing.
B. Yes, because the notice of the clause was reasonable, given it was in large red text.
C. No, because the notice of the clause was not contained in a contractual document but was instead on a sign.
D. No, because the notice of the clause came too late, after the contract was made and not at the time of contracting.
E. No, because an exclusion clause can only be incorporated by signature.

Question 3

A florist contracts with a vehicle dealership to purchase a new van for use in her business. A term of the contract for the van purchase is that the van will be "roadworthy". The florist takes delivery of the van but soon decides he would prefer a different model. He notices that the van has been supplied to him with insufficient brake fluid. It would cost £125 to refill the brake fluid.

What is the likely result of the breach of the term as to roadworthiness?

A. Because the term is likely to be a condition, the florist can terminate the contract.
B. Because the term is likely to be a warranty, the florist can terminate the contract.
C. Because the term is likely to be a warranty, the florist cannot terminate the contract.
D. Because the term is likely to be innominate, the florist can terminate the contract.
E. Because the term is likely to be innominate, the florist cannot terminate the contract.

6 Implied terms

6.1 Chapter overview

Chapter 5 considered the express terms which the parties agree to include in the contract. However, there are also a number of mechanisms by which additional terms can be included, despite not having been expressed by either party. These are known as implied terms. Implied terms can arise from a number of different sources: from legislation, from the courts, and from custom and usage. This chapter will first consider the two ways in which terms can be implied into all contracts of a particular type: by statute, and terms implied "in law" by the courts. It will then consider the two ways a term might be implied into one, particular contract that is the subject of a dispute: terms implied "in fact" by the courts and those implied by custom or trade usage.

6.2 Terms implied by statute

A considerable number of statutes and statutory instruments have the effect of implying terms into particular types of contracts. This section will consider the terms implied into contracts for goods and services by three important pieces of legislation:

- The Sale of Goods Act 1979;
- The Supply of Goods and Services Act 1982;
- The Consumer Rights Act 2015.

6.2.1 Terms implied in business-to-business or private sale contracts

All contracts for the supply of goods and/or services made before 1 October 2015, and all contracts that are not "consumer contracts" under the Consumer Rights Act 2015 made on or after 1 October 2015 will be subject to the terms implied under the Sale of Goods Act 1979 (SGA 1979) and the Supply of Goods and Services Act 1982 (SoGSA 1982). These terms are summarised in Table 6.1.

Attempts to exclude or limit liability for these implied terms will be governed by the provisions of the Unfair Contract Terms Act 1977, as discussed in Chapter 8.

DOI: 10.4324/9781032642161-9

Table 6.1 Implied terms in non-consumer contracts

Provision	Term	Explanation
S12 SGA 1979	The seller has the right to sell the goods	This term states that the seller owns the goods (has "title" to them) or has the permission of their owner to sell them on their owner's behalf.
S13 SGA 1979	The goods will correspond with the description given	Where goods are sold by description (for example, ecommerce where the buyer sees an image and/or description of the goods, rather than examining the goods themselves before purchase) the seller promises that the actual goods provided will match this description.
S14 SGA 1979	The goods will be of satisfactory quality (if sale is in the course of a business)	Satisfactory quality is a matter of fact in each case and will be dependent on context such as the price paid. The Act states that quality may include the following aspects: fitness for all the purposes for which goods of the kind in question are commonly supplied; appearance and finish; freedom from minor defects; safety; and durability.
S14 SGA 1979	The goods will be fit for a particular purpose (if sale is in the course of a business and the buyer makes a particular purpose for which the goods are being bought known to the seller)	The term will only be implied if the buyer makes the particular purpose known to the seller (although the term as to satisfactory quality will cover situations where goods are not fit for the usual purpose for which they are commonly supplied).
S13 SoGSA 1982	The service will be carried out with reasonable care and skill (if provided in the course of a business)	The standard expected will be that of a professional of ordinary competence and experience.

Provision	Term	Explanation
S14 SoGSA 1982	The service will be carried out within a reasonable time (if provided in the course of a business)	This term will only apply where the time for the service to be carried out is not fixed by the express terms of the contract.
S15 SoGSA 1982	The service will be carried out for a reasonable charge (if provided in the course of a business)	This term will only apply where the consideration for the service to be carried out is not fixed by the express terms of the contract.

6.2.2 Terms implied in business-to-consumer contracts

The Consumer Rights Act 2015 (CRA 2015) is a key piece of legislation that attempted to consolidate and expand the law relating to the sale and supply of goods and services as it related to "B2C" contracts: contracts between a business and a consumer.[1]

With regard to implied terms, the CRA 2015 applies to all contracts made on or after 1 October 2015 between a "trader" and a "consumer". These concepts are defined in the CRA 2015 as follows.[2]

In relation to these "consumer contracts", the CRA 2015 provides much the same terms in relation to the supply of goods and services as the previous legislation. Technically, the CRA does not "imply terms" but makes it a statutory provision that contracts are to be "treated as including" terms. In practice there appears to be no meaningful difference and so the CRA provisions are treated the same as implied terms under the previous legislation. The CRA 2015 also adds specific provisions relating to "digital content", which is defined as "data which are produced and supplied in digital form".[3] See Figure 6.1.

The provisions of the CRA 2015 are summarised in Table 6.2.

6.2.3 Remedies for consumers under the Consumer Rights Act 2015

Breach of terms implied by the SGA 1979 or the SoGSA 1982 is treated the same as any other contractual breach. However, where the CRA 2015 applies and goods, digital content, or services do not conform with the contract, special statutory remedies are available.

1 S1 Consumer Rights Act 2015.
2 S2 Consumer Rights Act 2015.
3 S2 Consumer Rights Act 2015.

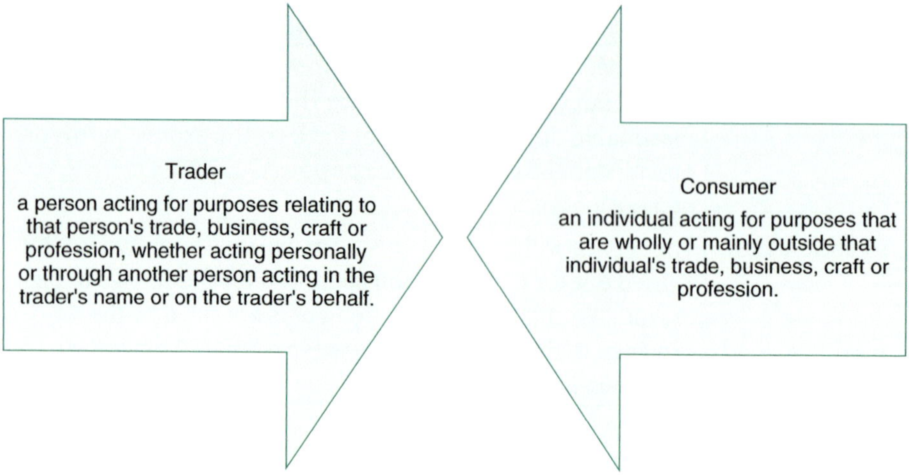

Figure 6.1 Definitions of traders and consumers

Table 6.2 Implied terms in consumer contracts

Provision	Term
S9 CRA 2015	The goods will be of satisfactory quality
S10 CRA 2015	The goods will be fit for any particular purpose made known to the trader
S11 CRA 2015	The goods will be as described
S17 CRA 2015	The trader will have the right to supply the goods
S34 CRA 2015	The digital content will be of satisfactory quality
S35 CRA 2015	The digital content will be fit for any particular purpose made known to the trader
S36 CRA 2015	The digital content will be as described
S41 CRA 2015	The trader will have the right to supply the digital content
S49 CRA 2015	The service will be performed with reasonable care and skill
S51 CRA 2015	A reasonable price will be paid for the service
S52 CRA 2015	The service will be performed within a reasonable time

In a consumer contract for the supply of goods, the consumer has an immediate short-term right to reject the goods and to receive a refund.[4] This right is available for 30 days after the goods have been delivered, unless the goods are of a kind that can reasonably be expected to perish after a shorter period.[5]

4 S20 Consumer Rights Act 2015.
5 S22 Consumer Rights Act 2015.

Unless the goods form a "commercial unit", this also allows the buyer to reject part of the goods, if only part do not conform to the contract for example, if a person buys five light bulbs and only four of the bulbs work.[6] A commercial unit is where goods only have commercial value as part of a larger whole – for example, a left shoe and a right shoe together make up a commercial unit, as either shoe is essentially useless on its own.

The second remedy available is the right to repair or replacement. The trader must, at their own cost and within a reasonable time limit, repair or replace the non-conforming goods.[7] The trader does not need to repair or replace if to do so is impossible or would be disproportionate compared to other remedies (e.g. a refund).

Finally, the consumer has the right to a price reduction or a final right to reject the goods. This arises where repair or replacement has failed, or is impossible or disproportionate, or has not been done within a reasonable time. At this point the consumer may receive either the full amount of the price or an appropriate partial refund to reflect the non-conformity of the goods.

Much of the same remedies apply to digital content.[8] There is also a specific remedy for where digital content causes damage to a device or other digital content belonging to the consumer due to a lack of reasonable care and skill on the part of the trader.[9] In this situation, the trader must repair the damage at their own cost, or compensate the consumer with an appropriate payment.

Consider the following scenario:

> Tom contracts with Unusual Unicorn, a software developer, to purchase software to help him organise his library of family photographs. Unusual Unicorn have failed to keep the download section of their website protected from hackers and a hacker has been able to replace the software download with a version infected with a virus. This causes significant damage to Tom's computer, requiring him to purchase replacement components.

Possibly Tom might be able to claim in the tort of negligence but this raises complex issues about duty of care and pure economic loss. Instead, Tom can claim under the CRA 2015 for the financial loss.

In relation to services provided which do not conform to the contract, the consumer has a right to require the trader to perform the service again, at their own

6 S21 Consumer Rights Act 2015.
7 S23 Consumer Rights Act 2015.
8 SS42–45 Consumer Rights Act 2015.
9 S46 Consumer Rights Act 2015.

cost and within a reasonable time (unless this is impossible).[10] If repeat performance is not available or not done within a reasonable time, the consumer is entitled to an appropriate reduction in price, up to and including a full refund where appropriate.[11]

6.3 Terms implied in law by the courts

When deciding to imply a term as part of its decision, the court can choose to imply the term "in fact" (implied into just the contract that is the subject of the case before the court) or "in law". The latter means that the term will be implied into all contracts falling under the law of England and Wales of that particular type. For example, a term might be implied in law into all contracts of employment. Because of the wider effect of such a decision, when implying a term in law the court will have regard to policy considerations and will only imply a term where the term is a necessary incident of a definable category of contractual relationship.[12] This is an intentionally vague test that allows judges to consider wider issues of reasonableness, fairness, and policy considerations.[13] For example, a term is implied into employment contracts that the employer will not conduct itself in such a corrupt and scandalous manner as to adversely affect the future career prospects of its (innocent) employees.[14]

6.4 Terms implied in fact by the courts

Unlike terms implied in law, terms implied in fact only apply to the particular contract that is the subject of the litigation. As such, the courts tend to take a more subjective approach to implying a term in fact, looking specifically at what the parties' intentions were at the time of contracting. While the court is willing to give effect to those unexpressed intentions, it is important to remember that the court will still be reluctant to imply a term unless it is needed. It is not the role of the court to make a contract for the parties, or to make a contract fairer or more convenient. As such, the starting point to imply a term in fact (and, for that matter, in law) is whether it is *necessary* – not merely whether it is reasonable.[15]

In order to establish whether it is necessary to imply a term in fact in order to make the contract work as the parties intended, the court can rely on one or both of two approaches.

10 S55 Consumer Rights Act 2015.
11 S56 Consumer Rights Act 2015.
12 *Scally v Southern Health and Social Services Board* [1992] 1 AC 294.
13 *Liverpool City Council v Irwin* [1977] AC 239.
14 *Malik v Bank of Credit and Commerce International SA (In Liquidation)* [1998] AC 20.
15 *Marks & Spencer Plc v BNP Paribas Securities Services Trust Co (Jersey) Ltd* [2015] UKSC 72.

Under the *business efficacy* approach, the court will ask whether the term is required to give efficacy to the contract in a business sense.[16] Note that the word is "efficacy" (the ability to produce an intended result), not "efficiency". The business efficacy approach in other words asks whether the term is necessary in order for the contract to make business sense or workable.

An alternative approach, although usually one which will lead to the same result, is that of the *officious bystander*. This involves a hypothetical bystander watching the contract being made, who suggests the term which could be implied. If *both* of the parties would have responded to the suggestion by saying "oh, of course" the term would be part of the contract, then it should be implied.[17] In other words, this test suggests an implied term should be included if it is so obvious to the parties it went without saying.

Even where one or both of tests are met, the term will still not be implied in two situations.

1. Where to do so would be incompatible with an express term of the contract.[18] The court must presume that the true agreement of the parties is that which is expressed within it, so will not imply a term which is directly contrary to that agreement.
2. Where the term implied cannot be formulated with sufficient clarity and precision.[19] The vaguer the term, the less likely it is to be implied into the contract.

6.5 Terms implied by custom or trade usage

Finally, a term may be implied into a contract because there is clear evidence that in that particular trade or place, such a term would always be included by implication. Arguably this is another form of implication in fact (because the custom was presumably known to the parties and so they intended to include the term) or in law (because it is being implied into all types of contracts in this particular trade). However, it is still considered a distinct form of implying terms. The test for whether a term will be implied in this manner is that it is more than a mere trade practice – the use of the term within the custom or trade is "notorious, certain and reasonable".[20]

16 *The Moorcock* (1889) 14 PD 64.
17 *Shirlaw v Southern Foundries (1926) Ltd* [1939] 2 KB 206.
18 *Marks & Spencer Plc v BNP Paribas Securities Services Trust Co (Jersey) Ltd* [2015] UKSC 72.
19 *Shell UK Ltd v Lostock Garage Ltd* [1976] 1 WLR 1187, 1197, 1201.
20 See for discussion *Cunliffe-Owen v Teather and Greenwood* [1967] 1 WLR 1421.

Chapter 6 Revision Points

Implied terms

- Implied by statute
  - B2B: Sale of Goods Act 1979 and Supply of Goods and Services Act 1982
  - B2C: Consumer Rights Act 2015
  - Key terms
    - Title to goods
    - Fit for particular purpose
    - Satisfactory quality
    - Reasonable care and skill
    - Reasonable time/price
  - Note CRA 2015 remedies
    - Short-term right to reject
    - Repair/replacement/repeat performance
    - Final rejection/price reduction
- Implied by courts: law
  - Implied into all contracts of a type
  - Matter of public policy
- Implied by courts: fact
  - Necessity not reasonableness
  - Business efficacy approach
  - Officious bystander approach
  - Must not contradict express term
  - Must be sufficiently clear and precise
- Implied by custom or trade usage
  - Notorious, certain, and reasonable
  - Not a mere trade practice

It is important to check your knowledge using the following Multiple Choice Questions.

Multiple Choice Questions

Question 1

A customer visits a car dealership looking to purchase a new car. She intends to use the car to commute to work, to drive her children to school, and for family trips at weekends. She tells the salesperson at the dealership that she owns a caravan and the car must be rated to tow that particular caravan model. Three months after purchasing the car, the customer discovers that this model of car cannot tow her model of caravan.

What claim does the customer have?

A. The car is not of satisfactory quality under the Consumer Rights Act 2015.
B. The car is not of satisfactory quality under the Sale of Goods Act 1979.
C. The car is not fit for purpose under the Consumer Rights Act 2015.
D. The car is not fit for purpose under the Sale of Goods Act 1979.
E. The car does not match its description under the Supply of Goods and Services Act 1982.

Question 2

During a contractual dispute in the High Court, a judge implies a term into the contract on the basis that it is required to make this particular contract make business sense.

How has the term been implied into the contract?

A. By statute
B. In law by the court
C. In fact by the court
D. By custom
E. By trade usage

7 The interpretation of terms

7.1 Chapter overview

Once the express and, where relevant, implied terms of the contract have been identified, the court must then consider what these terms mean. This is done through the process of interpretation (sometimes called "construction"), which determines the meaning and legal effect of the terms of the contract. All terms are open to interpretation – whether written or oral, express or implied, or conditions or warranties.

This chapter begins by explaining the objective approach taken by the court, with the aim of discerning the intention of the parties. It then goes on to consider the "unitary" approach which is today adopted by the courts when interpreting the terms of a contract. The chapter then turns to particular factors the court may have regard to during the process of interpretation: the wider context of the contract (often termed "the matrix of fact").

7.2 An objective approach to intention

As in many areas of contract law (for example, when determining agreement as discussed in Chapter 1, or when deciding if a statement is a term or a representation as discussed in Chapter 5) the court prefers to take an objective approach when determining what the parties intended by the term being interpreted. This means that rather than subjectively looking at what the parties themselves may have understood the term to mean, the court will instead consider what a reasonable person hearing the term would have understood it to mean.

7.3 The "unitary" approach to interpretation

The objective nature of interpretation historically led to a narrow approach where a court would limit itself to what was within the "four corners" of the contract. This was closely linked to the parol evidence rule (discussed in Chapter 5), which prevented parties from adducing evidence about the contract beyond the written contractual doctrine.

DOI: 10.4324/9781032642161-10

Just as the parol evidence rule has declined in importance, so the modern approach to contractual interpretation has become broader. It is often described in recent case law as a "unitary" approach, because it unites textualism (approaches based on the words of the contract itself) and contextualism (approaches based on the broader context in which the contract was made).[1] Under the unitary approach, the court must have regard to a number of factors, which are discussed in the following sections.[2]

- The language used in the disputed clause and its meaning;
- Other relevant provisions of the contract;
- The purpose of the clause and of the contract as a whole;
- The wider context in which the contract was made;
- Commercial common sense.

While this is a much broader approach to interpretation than the "four corners" approach, it is clear that the parties' subjective intentions remain irrelevant.

7.4 The language used

Practically speaking, the logical starting point is still the words of the clause itself. If the parties have set out how the term applies in clear and unambiguous language, the court is very unlikely to depart from this, because this is what the parties have agreed.[3] The usual starting point in establishing the meaning of the wording of the contract is to take the natural and ordinary meaning of the words. This does not necessarily mean how a word is defined in a dictionary, but how it is used in everyday life.[4]

Consider the following scenario:

> XYZ Enterprises contracted with Dimantium Construction for Dimantium to build new offices for XYZ. As part of the contract, it was stated that XYZ could deduct from the final payment of £2 million the cost of any work which was not completed on time, because of "negligence or default on the part of Dimantium". XYZ wanted to deduct the £150,000 cost of window glazing because this had been done late, after the contract stated it should be completed. Dimantium argue that "default" should be read as part of the reference to "negligence", to mean only work completed late because of Dimantium's own fault. The late window glazing was due to a late shipment of glass by another company rather than Dimantium's own negligence.

1 *Wood v Capita Insurance Services Ltd* [2017] UKSC 24.
2 *Arnold v Britton* [2015] UKSC 36.
3 *Melanesian Mission Trust Board v Australian Mutual Provident Society* [1997] 1 N.Z.L.R. 391.
4 *Robertson v French* (1803) 4 East 130.

The court would be very unlikely to give "default" this special meaning, relating to fault. In ordinary language, to "default" is to fail to do something (for example, defaulting on payment), and there is no reason to depart from this natural and ordinary meaning.[5]

7.4.1 Mistakes

Where the court is satisfied on the evidence before it that "something had gone wrong with the language" in that there was an obvious linguistic mistake, it can remedy that mistake through taking a different interpretation, contrary to the natural and ordinary meaning of the actual words used. It must not just be obvious to the hypothetical reasonable person that a mistake had been made in the language; it must also be clear to them what the parties actually meant, as this will be the interpretation the court uses instead.[6]

Consider the following scenario:

> Clive, who runs his own business building computers, contracts with Danny to build Danny a new gaming PC. The contract states that the computer will contain "500 2GB hard drives". The court hears that modern hard drives are usually around 500GB in size and that there is only space for a maximum of four or five hard drives in a standard desktop computer.

In a situation such as this, it is highly likely that the court would hold that the reasonable person would assume that a mistake had been made; and that it would be clear the numbers had been written the wrong way around – the contract should have specified two 500GB hard drives.

7.4.2 Ambiguous wording

Where a word or phrase is ambiguous, in that it is open to more than one (reasonable) interpretation, the court will determine the meaning by weighing the other factors relevant to the unitary approach. So if one meaning might make the term incompatible with other provisions of the contract, that would be a reason to take the other, compatible, interpretation.[7] Similarly, another way to resolve the ambiguity is to take the meaning which is more consistent with business common sense.[8]

5 See *ABC Electrification v Network Rail Infrastructure* [2020] EWCA Civ 1645 on which the facts of this scenario are based.
6 *Chartbrook Ltd v Persimmon Homes Ltd* [2009] UKHL 38.
7 *Egon Zehnder Ltd v Tillman* [2019] UKSC 32.
8 *Rainy Sky SA v Kookmin Bank* [2011] UKSC 50.

Consider the following scenario:

> A famous band entered into a contract to licence the rights to play their music. The contract referred to rights in a particular set of "records" recorded by the band. The other party to the contract argues that the contract does not apply to online music streaming, only to playing physical vinyl records of the band's music.

The court would be likely to find that the reference to "records" was using the phrase in the wider sense, to simply mean the particular albums the band had recorded which contained those songs. It would make little commercial sense to make an agreement about rights to music that only covered using that music on a niche format like vinyl records and which did not cover much more popular formats such as online streaming.[9]

The court may also use the *contra proferentum* rule, which construes a clause against the person who included it in the contract or who wishes to rely on it. This is likely to only be as a last resort in most cases, but the rule continues to have particular application in relation to exemption clauses and is discussed in Chapter 8 in this context.

7.5 Other relevant provisions

As already noted, the other provisions of the contract might be used to decide between competing interpretations, where only one interpretation is compatible with other terms. It is clear that in order to interpret any one given term, the court must consider the contract as a whole. Other provisions might also limit what other factors the court can give weight to, particularly in two situations:

1 The parties may have defined the meaning of a particular word or phrase elsewhere in the contract, making it likely that this was their true intention.
2 The parties may have included clauses which limit where else the court can look for evidence of their intentions. A notable example is an entire agreement clause (see Chapter 5).

7.6 The purpose of the clause and the contract

The court must not just look at the other clauses in the contract, but at the purpose of the contract as a whole. The court will interpret the contract in a way that is internally consistent, but that is also consistent with the purpose of making the

9 See *Pink Floyd Music Ltd v EMI Records Ltd* [2010] EWCA Civ 1429 on which the facts of this scenario are based.

agreement in the first place. The purpose of the contract also can help to suggest what meaning a particular term should have – for example, the price agreed for a service can be used to determine the extent of the service to be provided.[10]

7.7 The wider context

It is now well established that the court is allowed to look beyond the contract itself at what has come to be known as the "available background" or "matrix of fact" against which it was made.[11] This includes anything that was known or reasonably available to both parties at or before the time of contracting.[12] This wider context includes both the factual context (for example, the area of business in which the parties operated, common trade practice, shared cultural traditions of the parties) and the legal context (the relevant law that applied to the agreement at the time it was made).

However, there are limits on what can be considered. As a general principle, the court discourages parties disagreeing about background material that is not directly relevant to interpreting the clause. More specifically, the court will not allow evidence as part of the factual matrix which seeks to explore:

- The parties' subjective understanding;
- What was said or done during pre-contractual negotiations;
- Subsequent acts by the parties after the contract was made.

7.8 Commercial common sense

One key factor which interpretations must be checked against is what the courts term commercial (or business) common sense. This is quite a nebulous concept and the courts have been keen to limit its scope. Commercial common sense does not allow a court to rewrite a contract, or to adopt a strained interpretation of it, simply to make the contract more commercially reasonable. Nor does it operate with the benefit of hindsight – if an interpretation made commercial sense at the time the contract was made, it is not made invalid by the fact that the contract has in practice been commercially disastrous for a party.

7.9 The balancing exercise

By considering all of the factors outlined above, the court has to conduct a balancing exercise when choosing between different interpretations of a term. The unitary approach to interpretation has also been characterised as an "iterative"

10 See for example *Allen v Cameron* (1833) 1 Cr & M 832.
11 *Investors Compensation Scheme Ltd v West Bromwich Building Society* [1998] 1 WLR 896.
12 *Mostyn House Estate Management Co Ltd v Youde* [2022] EWCA Civ 929.

approach.[13] This means that where there are multiple suggested interpretations of a word, phrase, or term, the court will check each interpretation against the various factors that make up the approach. In many cases these factors will all point in the direction of one particular interpretation, but in other cases different factors may favour different interpretations. In this situation, the court has to decide which factors weigh most heavily in the balance.

7.9.1 Formality and quality of the agreement

One additional factor which can help to determine how this balance is struck is the formality and quality of the agreement. Where a contract is drawn up in a formal document, negotiated, and prepared with the assistance of skilled professionals (such as lawyers), the court is more likely to place particular reliance on the "textual" elements of the contract (i.e. the language used and the contract itself).[14] Vice versa, more informal agreements and/or those drawn up without legal advice might be more likely to be interpreted with particular emphasis placed on the factual matrix surrounding the making of the contract.

Chapter 7 Revision Points

Interpretation of terms

- Intention of the parties
- Established objectively
- Unitary approach
- Text
  - Language used
  - Other relevant provisions
- Context
  - Purpose of contract
  - Wider context
  - Commercial common sense
- Balancing exercise
  - Considering formality and quality of agreement

It is important to check your knowledge using the following Multiple Choice Question.

13 *Wood v Capita Insurance Services Ltd* [2017] UKSC 24.
14 *Wood v Capita Insurance Services Ltd* [2017] UKSC 24.

Multiple Choice Question

Question 1

The parties to an insurance contract are in dispute as to the meaning of a particular term. The contract insures a goods vehicle against damage caused by other drivers but under a term of the contract, the insurer will have no obligation to bear the cost of repairing any damage suffered if, at the time the damage occurred, the vehicle was under "excess load".

The insured vehicle was damaged in an accident. At the time the accident occurred, the vehicle had a small amount of goods onboard, well below the maximum weight the vehicle could transport. However, the driver of the vehicle was giving a lift to a fellow worker who was sat in the passenger seat.

The insurer argues that this was "excess load" because there was an extra person in the vehicle as well as the driver.

How will the court interpret the term?

A. The court will take the precise dictionary definitions of "excess" (more than necessary) and "load" (something being carried) and therefore interpret the term in favour of the insurer.
B. The court will look at what was said and done during pre-contractual negotiations between the parties, and use this factual matrix to interpret the term.
C. The court will take the ordinary and natural meaning of the words, having regard to commercial common sense. As a result, it is likely to interpret the term in favour of the insurer.
D. The court will take the ordinary and natural meaning of the words, having regard to commercial common sense. As a result, it is likely to interpret the term in favour of the owner of the insured vehicle.
E. The court will consider the subjective understanding of each party when interpreting the clause. As a result, it is likely to interpret the term in favour of the owner of the insured vehicle.

8 Exemption clauses and unfair contract terms

8.1 Chapter overview

Chapters 5–7 have focused on general principles which apply to the contents of the contract as a whole. However, certain particular types of term have attracted special attention from the law. These include terms in restraint of trade, covered in Chapter 12, and terms which purport to exclude or limit liability, or which are otherwise unfair, which are the subject of this chapter, Chapter 8.

After explaining why exemption clauses merit special treatment in contract law, this chapter covers three distinct ways in which such clauses are controlled. In order to rely on a clause attempting to exclude or limit liability, a party must show three things: that the clause was incorporated into the contract; that the wording of the clause covers the loss being limited or excluded; and that the term complies with relevant legislation. Because incorporation of terms was covered in depth in Chapter 5, the first section is very brief and you should refer to Chapter 5 on this point. The chapter then looks at interpretation in some detail before focusing in particular on the two key pieces of legislation which regulate exemption clauses (and unfair terms in consumer contracts): the Unfair Contract Terms Act 1977 and the Consumer Rights Act 2015.

8.2 Exemption clauses

When considering exemption clauses and other "unfair" terms, the law takes special note of such terms because of a risk of particularly unfair or onerous terms being forced onto one party by another. As such, much of the law in this area explicitly takes account of the relative bargaining power of the parties. It is more likely that the court will refuse to uphold an exclusion clause where it is being relied on by the stronger party in an unequal relationship, such as a large business against an individual consumer, than the same term in a relatively equal commercial relationship between two businesses.

DOI: 10.4324/9781032642161-11

8.3 Incorporation of exemption clauses

The different methods of incorporating a term were considered in Chapter 5: through signature, through reasonable notice, and through a consistent course of dealing. The same law applies to incorporation of exemption clauses. Because exemption clauses are particularly onerous clauses, they usually require a relatively high degree of notice to be incorporated through this method.

It should be noted that where a party misrepresents the meaning and effect of an exemption clause, that party cannot rely on the clause. For example, if person A tells person B that the document they are signing contains no terms excluding liability for negligence, and the document does actually contain such a term, it will not be validly incorporated due to the fraudulent statement.[1]

8.4 Interpretation of exemption clauses

Before the creation of the legislation covered in the following sections of this chapter, interpretation was, alongside incorporation, the only way in which the courts could regulate exemption clauses. As such, a number of cases saw terms interpreted in a rather strained way in an attempt to account for the unequal bargaining power of the parties. It is unlikely that many of these cases would be decided on the same grounds today, both because the rules relating to interpretation of terms have developed and because the courts have less need to creatively interpret seemingly unfair exemption clauses, because these clauses will often be ineffective due to the legislation in the area.

Two key principles of interpretation do, however, remain important. Before reviewing the law on interpretation, consider the following scenario:

> Jiro runs a business hiring out bouncy castles and other inflatable toys, for use at children's parties. When customers hire from Jiro, he asks them to sign a contract which contains the following clauses:
>
> > Jiro is not liable for any loss or damage to the customer's person or property, howsoever caused, arising from the use of the hired equipment.
> >
> > If, at any time during the hire period, the customer allows use of the bouncy castle by adults (those above school age), Jiro will not be liable for any damage caused.

Harry hires a bouncy castle from Jiro for his son Iain's seventh birthday. Because of the negligence of Jiro in inflating the bouncy castle, it is not fully inflated and Iain

1 *Curtis v Chemical Cleaning and Dyeing Co* [1951] 1 KB 805.

falls off the bouncy castle and injures himself. After the party is over, Iain's older brother, Karl, has a go on the bouncy castle. Karl is 17 and left school a few months ago. He now attends sixth-form college. Due to the ongoing problem with the inflation of the bouncy castle, Karl also falls off and injures himself.

8.4.1 The clause must cover the loss

As a simple rule, it must be shown that the wording of the clause actually covers the loss being claimed. In the scenario given above, Jiro has purported to exclude liability for loss or damage to the *customer's person or property*. This might, as a matter of interpretation, cover any injury suffered by Harry, who hired the bouncy castle – but it cannot be relied on to prevent a claim in negligence in Iain's name. Iain is not the customer, so the clause does not cover the actual loss.

Historically, there was a suggestion that in order to exclude liability for negligence, this had to be stated expressly within the clause. However, the modern position is that words wide enough to cover all forms of liability include liability for negligence – so a phrase such as "howsoever caused" is unlikely to be interpreted to not cover liability in negligence.[2]

8.4.2 Interpretation *contra proferentem*

Where the words of an exemption clause are ambiguous (capable of having more than one meaning), the court will interpret the clause *contra proferentem*. This means against (*contra*) the person proffering, i.e. relying on, the clause (the *proferens*).[3]

Returning to Jiro's scenario, it could be argued that the phrase "adults (those above school age)" is ambiguous. Jiro is likely to argue that it means anyone over the age all children must attend school, which is the last day of the school year in which they turn 16. That would mean the clause might exclude liability for Karl's injury. However, it would also be reasonable to assume that the word "adults" refers to those aged 18 and above, the usual age of majority – and that in any event, children are required to continue in education and training until their 18th birthday, albeit that this might be through college or an apprenticeship rather than in a school. Because Jiro is the person relying on the clause, the court will take the meaning less favourable to Jiro, which is that the clause only excludes liability for those aged 18+ using the equipment.

8.5 The Unfair Contract Terms Act 1977

The Unfair Contract Terms Act 1977 (UCTA 1977) is a statute that was passed specifically to regulate the use of contractual exemption clauses. The Act only applies to clauses which exclude or restrict liability.

2 See for example *Aprile SpA v Elin Maritime Ltd (The Elin)* [2019] EWHC 1001 (Comm).
3 *Houghton v Trafalgar Insurance Co* [1954] 1 QB 247.

The Act applies to all clauses that relate to "business liability" – things done in the course of a business, or from the occupation of premises used for business purposes.[4] "Business" includes a profession and the activities of any government department or local or public authority.[5] However, the Act does not apply to consumer contracts, because these are now governed by the Consumer Rights Act 2015 (CRA 2015), explained later in this chapter (UCTA 1977 did apply to consumer contracts prior to CRA 2015).

As such, as a general rule of thumb exemption clauses in "B2B" contracts (contracts between two businesses) are governed by UCTA 1977, whereas exemption clauses in "B2C" contracts (contracts between a trader and a consumer) are governed by CRA 2015. To return to the example of Jiro's clauses given in section 8.4, this contract would be governed by CRA 2015 rather than UCTA 1977.

There are also specific categories of contract excluded by UCTA 1977, including contracts of insurance, contracts relating to interests in land, and international supply contracts.

8.5.1 Liability for negligence

Under UCTA 1977 a person cannot use a contract term or notice to exclude or restrict his or her liability for death or personal injury resulting from negligence. Negligence in the context of UCTA 1977 includes:

- Express or implied obligations under the contract to take reasonable care and/or skill[6];
- Common law duties to take reasonable care;
- The duty of care from occupiers to visitors, imposed by the Occupier's Liability Act 1957.

Where a term purports to exclude or restrict liability for any other loss or damage other than death or personal injury resulting from negligence, it will only be effective in so far as it satisfies the "reasonableness test" which is discussed below.

In practice, it is perfectly possible that a clause will seek to exclude multiple types of loss. Thus a clause might purport to exclude liability "for death, personal injury, damage to property or financial loss caused by negligence". In such a scenario, the court is able to sever the part of the clause prohibited outright (in this example, the words "death" and "personal injury"). As such, if the clause with the offending words removed meets the reasonableness test, it may still prove effective to exclude or limit liability for other types of loss.[7]

4 S1(3) Unfair Contract Terms Act 1977.
5 S14 Unfair Contract Terms Act 1977.
6 For example, this would include the implied term that the supplier of a service will carry it out with reasonable care and skill from S13 Supply of Goods and Services Act 1982.
7 For an example of where this occurred, see *Goodlife Foods Ltd v Hall Fire Protection Ltd* [2017] EWHC 767 (TCC).

8.5.2 Contractual liability: general

As well as tortious liability in negligence, UCTA 1977 also covers clauses which attempt to exclude or limit liability for breach of contract – but only where one party deals on the other's written standard terms of business.[8] This means that UCTA 1977 does not apply if the contract is bespoke, or if substantial variations are made during the negotiating process. Where standard terms are used, UCTA 1977 makes any clause which excludes or restricts liability for any breach of contract subject to the test of reasonableness.[9]

The Act also covers terms which allow a party to render substantially different performance or to render no performance at all – so it would, for example, cover a clause that allows one party to unilaterally change what they are expected to do under the contract (i.e. redrafting the contract to avoid breach).

8.5.3 Contractual liability: specific

UCTA 1977 contains specific provisions which relate to the terms implied by the Sale of Goods Act 1979, which were discussed in Chapter 6.[10] The seller cannot exclude or restrict liability for breach of the implied term as to title (that the seller owns or has the right to sell the goods) at all.[11]

In relation to the following implied terms, the test of reasonableness will apply[12]:

- That the goods will conform with their description;
- That the goods will be of satisfactory quality;
- That the goods will be fit for any particular purpose.

It should be noted that UCTA 1977 does not apply to the similar provisions under the Consumer Rights Act 2015 (CRA 2015), because Part 2 of the CRA 2015 contains its own provisions relating to unfair terms in consumer contracts, considered below.

8.5.4 The reasonableness test

As stated, a number of types of term are subject under UCTA 1977 to a test of reasonableness, including clauses exempting liability for:

- Negligently caused damage other than personal injury or death;
- Breach of contract where one party deals on the other's standard terms;
- Breach of implied terms under the Sale of Goods Act 1979.

8 S3(1) Unfair Contract Terms Act 1977.
9 S3(2)(a) Unfair Contract Terms Act 1977.
10 These provisions also relate to terms implied under the Supply of Goods (Implied Terms) Act 1973.
11 S6(1) Unfair Contract Terms Act 1977.
12 S6(1A) Unfair Contract Terms Act 1977.

The reasonableness test is that the term must be "a fair and reasonable one to be included having regard to the circumstances which were, or ought reasonably to have been, known to or in the contemplation of the parties when the contract was made".[13] Therefore the court must decide whether the term was fair and reasonable in this particular case, between these particular parties, without the benefit of hindsight as to what has happened since.

The burden of proof lies on the person claiming that the clause is reasonable, i.e. the party seeking to rely on the exemption clause.[14] What is reasonable is decided on a case-by-case basis, but over time the law has identified a number of factors that will be relevant to this determination.

The statutory factors

UCTA 1977 provides a set of particular factors which apply in cases relating to exempting liability for statutory implied terms, but this list has also been used in cases relating to other types of clauses such as those excluding liability for negligence. The factors stated in the statute are:[15]

- The relative strength of the bargaining positions of the parties;
- Whether one party received an inducement to agree to the term, or had the option to enter a similar contract with others that did not include the term;
- Whether the other party knew or ought reasonably to have known of the existence of the term (having regard to trade custom and previous dealings);
- Where the clause applies when some condition is not complied with, whether compliance was practicable at the time of contracting;
- Whether the goods were manufactured, processed, or adapted to the special order of the customer.

Factors from case law

Cases on UCTA 1977 have expanded on the list above. The courts have based their decision on whether a clause was reasonable by referring to factors such as:

- Not just whether a party knew of the term, but whether they understood its significance;
- Whether the parties had access to legal advice when making the contract;
- The wider context of the contract as a whole;
- The availability of insurance (the term being less likely to be reasonable if insurance was easily available to the party excluding liability, and vice versa).
- Whether including a term of this type was standard practice within the industry

13 S11(2) Unfair Contract Terms Act 1977.
14 S11(5) Unfair Contract Terms Act 1977.
15 Schedule 2 Unfair Contract Terms Act 1977.

Limitation clauses

The Act itself states that where the clause limits liability to a specified sum of money, rather than excluding liability entirely, the court should look specifically at two further factors: the resources available to the limiting party to meet that liability should it arise, and the availability of insurance.[16] Case law has established a more general principle, that the law will in general look more favourably on clauses that merely limit liability rather than exclude it outright.[17]

Consider the following scenario:

> Jim is a model railway enthusiast who occasionally builds model trains for other enthusiasts, usually charging around £100 to do so. Kenneth asks Jim to build a model train for use in his large commercial model railway, which is open to the public. Jim is keen to do the work, as Kenneth is offering a large fee of £1,000, but this is a much bigger project than he is used to. He negotiates with Kenneth that he will accept the contract if a term is included limiting Jim's liability to £2,000. When Kenneth uses the train, the electronics in his railway undergo a power surge due to Jim not properly installing a particular fuse. This causes extensive damage to the railway which Kenneth states will cost £100,000 to fully repair.

It is likely that on these facts the clause would be held to be reasonable. Jim owns a small business, and does not have the resources to meet liability of hundreds of thousands of pounds. Furthermore, it would be easier for Kenneth to insure his own machinery against damage than it would be for Jim to obtain insurance protecting him from liability.

8.6 The Consumer Rights Act 2015

CRA 2015 replaced UCTA 1977 in relation to exemption clauses contained within "consumer contracts". As explained in Chapter 6, a consumer contract is one between a trader and a consumer, as defined by the CRA 2015.[18] The CRA 2015 uses different language to UCTA 1977. Rather than reasonableness, it relies on a concept of fairness.

8.6.1 Scope of the 2015 Act

The other key difference between the two Acts is that CRA 2015 can apply to a wider category of terms – it applies to all terms in consumer contracts (with one key exception as explained below) rather than just terms excluding or limiting liability.

16 S11(5) Unfair Contract Terms Act 1977.
17 *Ailsa Craig Fishing Co Ltd v Malvern Fishing Co Ltd (The Strathallan)* [1983] 1 WLR 964.
18 S2 Consumer Rights Act 2015.

The exception is so-called core terms. These are the terms which specify the main subject matter of the contract. The Act also does not allow assessment of the appropriateness of the price payable under the contract, so it is not possible to argue a term requiring payment is unfair because the price being paid for the goods or service does not represent good value.[19] However, wider aspects relating to price are covered. For example, a consumer could bring a claim that a term requiring payment of 50% of the price in event of cancellation was unfair.

8.6.2 Terms which must be regarded as unfair

CRA 2015 prohibits two particular terms.

1. A term which excludes or restricts liability for death or personal injury resulting from negligence;[20]
2. A term of a contract to supply goods, digital content, or services is not binding on the consumer to the extent that it would exclude the statutory liabilities included in the contract by the CRA 2015 (e.g. satisfactory quality, service to be provided with reasonable care and skill).[21]

8.6.3 Terms which may be regarded as unfair

For all other non-core terms not prohibited outright, the requirement is that such terms are fair. Unfair terms are not binding on consumers. A term is unfair if, contrary to the requirement of good faith, it causes a significant imbalance in the parties' rights and obligations under the contract to the detriment of the consumer.[22] This is a single test, but it includes three distinct factors, which will now be discussed in turn:

Significant imbalance in the parties' rights and obligations under the contract

It is crucial to understand that this part of the test applies to the term in question, rather than the contract as a whole. The court is not looking at whether the contract as a whole is a "bad bargain" but whether this particular term has the effect of causing a significant imbalance between the parties' rights and obligations. European jurisprudence (the CRA 2015 test is based heavily on existing EU law) suggests the starting point should be to look at what the position of the consumer would be without the term.[23]

However, to decide the effect of the term the court must then also look at the wider context. A seemingly imbalanced term might actually be balanced elsewhere in the contract; for example, a term might allow the trader to change the

19 S64 Consumer Rights Act 2015.
20 S65 Consumer Rights Act 2015.
21 SS33, 47 and 57 Consumer Rights Act 2015.
22 S62 Consumer Rights Act 2015.
23 *Aziz v Caixa d'Estalvis de Catalunya, Tarragona i Manresa (Catalunyacaiza)* EU:C:2013:164.

price of a service after the contract is made, but this might be balanced by another term which allows the consumer to cancel the contract at any time.

To the detriment of the consumer

This is a relatively straightforward part of the test. Clearly, if a term was imbalanced in favour of the consumer, it would not be "unfair" within the meaning of the CRA 2015.

Contrary to the requirement of good faith

"Good faith" is another legacy of the European basis for the test. English and Welsh contract law has not historically recognised a doctrine of "good faith". Practically speaking, the idea of "good faith" significantly overlaps with the idea of "fairness" under the test. Once the consumer has established there is a significant imbalance to their detriment, the question becomes whether that imbalance is unfair.

In deciding this, the court must have regard to the nature of the subject matter of the contract and all the circumstances existing when the term was agreed and to all of the other terms of the contract or of any other contract on which it depends.[24] The nature of the subject matter of the contract means that the court could consider whether this was a standard consumer contract (such as purchasing mass market goods in a shop) or a more specialised contract (such as for building a costly and unique building) where it might be fairer to limit or exclude certain liability. The court may also look at common practice in the area and how unusual the clause was. Regarding the idea of "all the circumstances existing", this might include whether the customer was particularly vulnerable and/or placed under particular high pressure sales tactics, or where a consumer was not given an opportunity to read or understand the term.

8.6.4 "Grey list" terms

The CRA 2015 itself sets out an illustrative list of terms which *may* be unfair. This is intended as an indicative example – the list is not exhaustive, nor is it decisive. Terms which appear on the list may not be unfair in a particular contract; while other terms in contracts may be unfair even though they do not appear on the list. This has led to the term being described as a "grey list" (as opposed to a "black list" of prohibited terms).

The grey list includes, among others, terms which:

- Exclude or limit the trader's liability;
- Allow the trader to retain sums paid when they themselves cancel the contract;

24 S62(5) Consumer Rights Act 2015.

- Require the consumer to pay a disproportionately high sum for cancelling or breaching the contract;
- Automatically extend the contract without the consumer's express consent;
- Allow the trader to vary the terms of the contract after it is made;
- Constitute "entire agreement" clauses (see Chapter 5).

Chapter 8 Revision Points

Exemption clauses

- Incorporation (see Chapter 5)
  - By signature
  - By reasonable notice
  - By consistent course of dealing
- Interpretation
  - Clause must cover the loss
  - Interpretation contra proferentem
- Legislation B2B: UCTA 1977
  - Cannot exclude:
    - Death/personal injury by negligence
    - Some implied terms
  - Can exclude if reasonable:
    - Other loss by negligence
    - Contract liability if standard form
    - Some implied terms
  - Reasonableness test
- Legislation B2C: CRA 2015
  - Does not apply to "core" terms
  - Cannot exclude:
    - Death/personal injury by negligence
    - Implied terms
  - All other terms subject to fairness test:
    - Imbalance in rights and obligations
    - Contrary to requirement of good faith

It is important to check your knowledge using the following Multiple Choice Questions.

Multiple Choice Questions

Question 1

A university asks all students to sign a contract on commencing their studies. Clause 34 of the contract excludes all liability on behalf of the university for any personal injury suffered by students while on campus. Clause 49 of the contract excludes all liability for breach of contract on behalf of the university.

How will legislation govern the exclusion clauses in this contract?

A. The Consumer Rights Act 2015 will automatically hold both Clause 34 and Clause 49 to be unfair.
B. The Consumer Rights Act 2015 will hold Clause 34 to be automatically unfair. Clause 49 will be subject to the fairness test.
C. The Unfair Contract Terms Act 1977 will hold Clause 34 to be automatically void. Clause 49 will be subject to the reasonableness test.
D. The Unfair Contract Terms Act 1977 will hold Clause 34 to be subject to the reasonableness test. Clause 49 will be automatically void.
E. The legislation will have no effect because neither clause has been validly incorporated into the contract.

Question 2

A multinational confectionery company negotiates an agreement with a national chain of supermarkets, under which the confectionery company will supply the supermarkets with large quantities of chocolate bars for sale. As part of the contract negotiated between lawyers representing each company, it is agreed that the confectionary company will not be liable for any financial loss caused to the supermarket as a result of late delivery. Six months into the agreement, the confectionary company delivers a consignment of chocolate bars later than agreed. The supermarket chain wishes to sue for breach of contract.

Will the exclusion clause in the contract prevent a claim?

A. No, because the clause is automatically void under relevant legislation.

B. No, because the clause, contrary to the requirement of good faith, causes a significant imbalance in the parties' rights and obligations under the contract to the detriment of the consumer.

C. No, because the clause is not a fair and reasonable one to be included having regard to the circumstances which were, or ought reasonably to have been, known to or in the contemplation of the parties when the contract was made.

D. Yes, because the clause does not cause a significant imbalance in the parties' rights and obligations under the contract to the detriment of the consumer.

E. Yes, because the clause is a fair and reasonable one to be included having regard to the circumstances which were, or ought reasonably to have been, known to or in the contemplation of the parties when the contract was made.

PART 3

Vitiating elements

9 Misrepresentation

9.1 Chapter overview

During the pre-contractual stages, various statements might be made by the parties. These statements may, in some cases, form the terms of the contract, while in other cases, they amount to representations (see Chapter 5). If a representation is proven to be untrue, it may constitute misrepresentation. To successfully pursue a claim for misrepresentation, these statements must be actionable. This chapter considers the different requirements the claimant must demonstrate to establish a representation is an actionable misrepresentation. Once established, the actionable statement should be categorised to determine the remedies available to the innocent party.

9.2 Actionable misrepresentations

A misrepresentation refers to a false statement. The statement must be factual and made during the pre-contractual negotiation stages. This statement must induce the innocent party to enter into a contract, and as a result of this inducement, the innocent party suffers loss. To sue for misrepresentation, it must be actionable. In assessing whether a statement is actionable, certain requirements must be satisfied, which are set out in Figure 9.1.

9.2.1 Unambiguous false statement

The first requirement is that it must be unambiguous and pertain to an untrue (i.e. false) statement.[1] A false statement is a clear statement which is not substantially true.[2]

9.2.2 Statement of fact or law

It must be a statement of fact rather than a statement of opinion[3] or an honest statement about a future intention.[4] However, lying about a current opinion or

1 The test is whether the statement is "substantially correct" – see *Avon Insurance plc v Swire Fraser* [2000] 1 All ER (Comm) 573.
2 See *Avon Insurance plc v Swire Fraser* [2000] 1 All ER (Comm) 573.
3 *Bisset v Wilkinson* [1927] AC 177.
4 See *Wales v Wadham* [1977] 1 WLR 199.

DOI: 10.4324/9781032642161-13

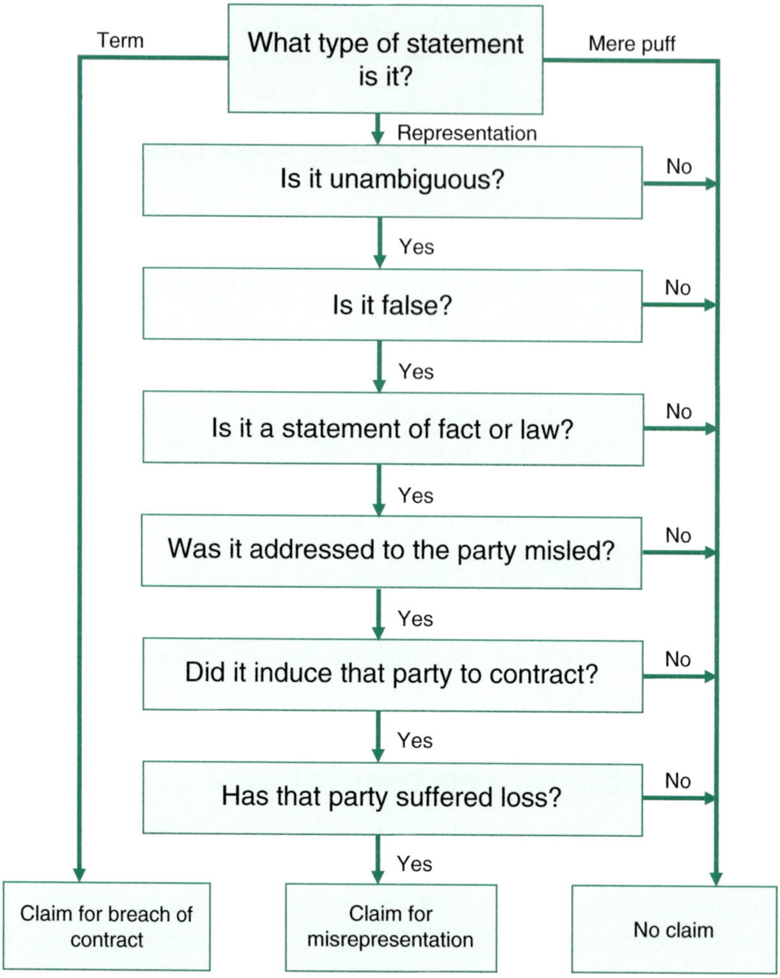

Figure 9.1 Actionable misrepresentations

intention constitutes a statement of fact, because it is a false statement of fact that the statement maker holds that opinion or intention.[5] Where an expert gives their opinion, it may constitute a statement of fact due to their specialist knowledge.[6]

When assessing whether it is a statement of fact, it must be noted that silence will not, in some cases, amount to a misrepresentation as there is no general duty to disclose. Contract law usually recognises the principle of *caveat emptor* – buyer beware. However, there are some exceptions to this rule, such as where a party's

5 *Edgington v Fitzmaurice* (1885) 29 Ch D 459.
6 *Esso Petroleum Co Ltd v Mardon* [1976] QB 801.

conduct can be considered to be a statement of fact in itself.[7] Other exceptions include partially correct statements, known as half-truths,[8] and situations where the circumstances have changed, i.e. true at the time of making the statement but false by the time the contract is concluded.

Some contracts rely on the principle of *uberrimaie fidei*, requiring full disclosure of all material facts. An example of this is insurance contracts, which place the duty on the insured person to disclose all relevant information. Although there is no duty to check, there are circumstances where it would be reasonable to check (for example, if it involves a larger amount of money and a commercial venture).

9.2.3 Addressed to the claimant and relied on by the claimant

In addition to identifying the statement as fact, it must be addressed to the claimant, who relied on it when entering the contract and subsequently suffered a loss. While there is no duty to check the truth of each statement made,[9] this depends on the context.[10] If the claimant has relied on their own investigations, actionability will fail on this component[11] unless the misrepresentation is fraudulent.[12] The reliance on the statement must have induced the party to enter the contract. In cases of innocent or negligent misrepresentation (see below) the test for inducement is a "but for" test. It must be said that but for the misrepresentation, the claimant would not have entered into the contract.[13] In cases of fraudulent misrepresentation, the test is easier to meet – the claimant only has to show that the representation was "actively present to his mind".[14]

Consider this scenario

Thomas, an entrepreneur, decides to buy a laundrette. Thomas contacts Vincent the current owner to discuss the potential sale. The next day, Thomas meets Vincent at the premises and notices the laundrette is quiet. Vincent assures him that the laundrette is normally "very busy because of the offices across the road". Vincent is aware the offices will be demolished in a few months which will inevitably have an impact on the laundrette's revenue.

A few months after the sale, the offices are demolished, and because of this, there are very few customers that use the laundrette. Thomas later finds out that the offices have been demolished and is furious that he was not told about this by Vincent. Can Thomas bring a claim against Vincent for misrepresentation?

7 *Spice Girls v Aprilla World Service* [2000] EMLR 478.
8 *With v O'Flanagan* [1936] 1 All ER 727.
9 *Redgrave v* Hurd [1881] 20 Ch D 1.
10 If commercial more reasonable to check – see *Smith v Eric S Bush* [1990] UKHL 1.
11 *Attwood v Small* (1838) 7 ER 684.
12 *S Pearson v Dublin Corp* [1907] AC 351, 353.
13 *BV Nederlandse Industrie Van Eiprodukten v Rembrandt Enterprises Inc* [2019] EWCA Civ 596.
14 *Edgington v Fitzmaurice* (1885) 29 Ch D 459.

Thomas should be advised that he has two potential claims. The first is for breach of contract as the statements may amount to terms and can be incorporated into the contract as terms (see Chapter 5) as it will be easier to prove in practice. However, in these circumstances Thomas will be best advised to pursue a claim for misrepresentation, because it is unlikely a statement about how busy the laundrette usually is will be precise enough to form a term.

To sue for misrepresentation the statement needs to be actionable misrepresentation. For Vincent's statement to be actionable it needs to be clear and false. Vincent's statement about the laundrette being "very busy" is now clearly false and relates to a statement of fact. Because Vincent has expertise as the owner of the business, it is not likely to be considered merely a statement of opinion.

It is technically true at the time of the statement that the laundrette is very busy, but this is because of the offices across the road, which is misleading as Vincent is aware they will be demolished, which can be construed as misleading. Vincent is under no general duty to disclose, but Vincent's silence on this point, given he has said the offices usually provide a lot of customers, amounts to a half-truth.[15]

Thomas is not under a duty to investigate, although it may be reasonable for him to do so considering it is a business venture and the amount of money involved.[16] As a result, Thomas has relied on the statement about the laundrette trade which as a result has induced him to enter the contract and as a result, Thomas has suffered loss. Vincent's statement as to a "wonderful opportunity" is clearly a mere puff, and Thomas should be advised that this will fail the actionability criteria for his claim to be successful.

9.3 Categories of misrepresentations

Once it has been established that the statement is actionable, it is important to establish the type of misrepresentation to work out the relevant remedies available. There are three different types of misrepresentation:

9.3.1 Fraudulent

This refers to a situation where the statement maker *knowingly*, i.e. with the knowledge that it is false, provides false information; or does so *without belief* in its truth or *recklessly*, careless as to whether the statement made is true or false.[17]

15 A statement which is true that misrepresents the whole situation – see *Dimmock v Hallett* (1866) LR 2 Ch App 21.

16 If Thomas can prove that Vincent's statement was fraudulent, investigation will not be required in any event.

17 See *Derry v Peek* (1889) 14 App Cas 337.

9.3.2 Negligent

The second category of misrepresentation is negligent, specifically a non-fraudulent or careless statement, but one which does not qualify as innocent (see below). There are two types of negligent misrepresentation:

- Negligent misstatement under common law principles derived from the *tort of negligence*. Not strictly part of contract law, this claim requires that a duty of care is established in the first instance.[18]
- *Negligent misrepresentation under the Misrepresentation Act 1967*, which is usually used in a contractual context if a claim for fraudulent misrepresentation is unavailable.

There are differences between a common law tortious claim for negligent misstatement and a statutory claim. In the context of a common law claim under the tort of negligence, the burden of proof is on the claimant. Conversely, under a statutory claim, this is reversed, and the burden of proof rests with the defendant (to show that the statement was made innocently rather than negligently). Furthermore, there is no need to prove a special relationship under the statutory claim, but this is essential under the tortious claim for negligent misstatement.

As such, a contractual claim under the Misrepresentation Act 1967 is usually preferable but, it is only available where the misrepresentation led to a contract being made.[19] There is no need to establish the existence of a contract to bring a claim in tort.

9.3.3 Innocent

Innocent misrepresentation refers to the types of misrepresentation that are neither non-fraudulent nor negligent. It must be shown that the statement maker:

1. Believed the statement to be true, up to the time the contract was made; and
2. Had reasonable grounds for that belief.[20]

In the preceding scenario it was established that the statement relating to the laundrette trade was actionable. It is now important to consider which category Thomas' claim for misrepresentation would fall under. Thomas should be advised to sue using the contractual version of misrepresentation rather than in tort as there is no need to prove a special relationship, and the burden of proof is on the defendant. It might be difficult to establish that Vincent knowingly misled Thomas, so it may be advisable to sue in negligent rather than fraudulent misrepresentation.

18 *Hedley Byrne & Co. Ltd v Heller Partners Ltd* [1964] AC 465.
19 S2(1) Misrepresentation Act 1967.
20 S2(1) Misrepresentation Act 1967. See *Redgrave v Hurd* [1881] 20 Ch D 1 for an example of an innocent misrepresentation.

9.4 Remedies

The discovery of an actionable misrepresentation will render the contract voidable. In effect, this means that the contract will remain valid until the innocent party decides to set the contract aside. The innocent party will have a choice as to whether to avoid the contract, in other words, to rescind the contract by making it clear that they are not bound by it, or alternatively, they may continue (affirm) the contract.[21]

9.4.1 Rescission

Rescission is available for all types of misrepresentation. Rescission is an equitable remedy, which means that it is discretionary. It has the effect of rewinding the transaction, setting aside the contract and restoring the parties to their original pre-contractual position. However, there are bars to rescission. For instance, the innocent party may lose their right to set the contract aside due to a lapse of time (time taken to set the contract aside)[22] or if a third party acquires rights under the contract.[23] Rescission will also not be granted where it is not possible to substantially restore the parties to their pre-contractual positions (for example, where the subject matter of the contract has subsequently been destroyed).

9.4.2 Indemnity

Additionally, a financial payment, also known as an indemnity, is available alongside rescission as a remedy to compensate for a loss suffered by the representee. This remedy is only applicable to obligations to third parties that were incurred as a necessary or inevitable result of the contract.

9.4.3 Damages

It must be noted that remedies for negligent misstatement will be based on the tortious measure for awarding damages. This means that damages for misrepresentation seek to place a party back in the position they were in before the misrepresentation occurred (i.e. as if they had never entered the contract), rather than on the usual "expectation" basis used in contract law (i.e. as if the contract had been performed successfully). See Chapter 16 for a detailed discussion of contractual damages.

The remedies available for each type of misrepresentation differ depending on the types of misrepresentation outlined in Figure 9.2.

21 See *Long v Lloyd* [1958] 2 All ER 402, where the innocent party's right to rescind was lost when driven after P became aware of misrepresentation.
22 See *Leaf v International Galleries* [1950] 1 All ER 693 for an example where it was held five years was unreasonable delay.
23 *Phillips v Brooks* [1919] 2 KB 243.

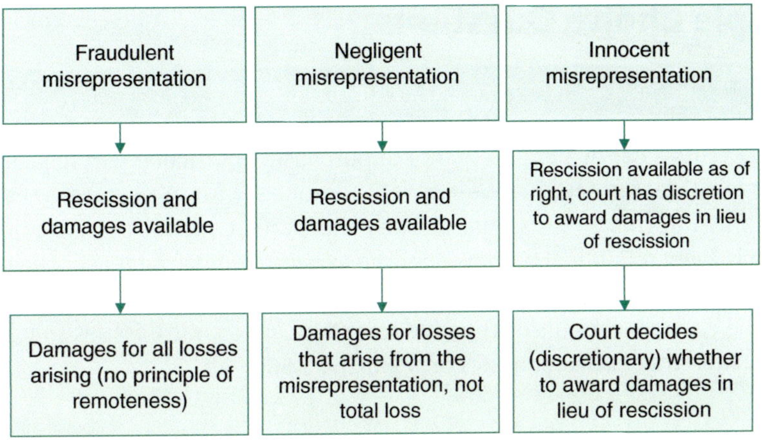

Figure 9.2 Categories of misrepresentation

Chapter 9 Revision Points

Misrepresentation

- Is the statement a term or representation?
- If the statement is not true:
    - Term? Sue for breach of contract
    - Representation? Sue for misrepresentation
- Misrepresentation must be actionable
    - False
    - Statement of fact
    - Reliance/inducement
    - Suffer loss
- Categories
    - Fraudulent: (knowingly, recklessly without belief in its truth)
    - Negligent misstatement under common law (tort), or S2(1) Misrepresentation Act 1967
    - Innocent
- Remedies
    - Differ depending on type of misrepresentation

It is important to check your knowledge using the following Multiple Choice Questions.

Multiple Choice Questions

Question 1

Brenda visits a car dealer and wants to purchase a particular vintage car from a specialist dealer. She has seen a reconditioned Triumph car. Leroy, a sales assistant, informs Brenda that he has the perfect model available for her which is "very reliable". He shows her the car and Brenda purchases the car for £10,000. A few weeks after purchasing the car, Brenda finds out from a friend that the car is in fact unreliable due to various mechanical issues that would be obvious to a car dealer and is only worth £1,500.

Which of the following best describes the legal position?

A. The statement made by Leroy is a negligent misrepresentation, so rescission is not available.
B. The statement made by Leroy is an innocent representation, so damages are not available as of right.
C. The statement made by Leroy is an innocent representation, so rescission is available.
D. The statement made by Leroy is a mere puff and there is no claim for misrepresentation
E. The statement made by Leroy is a negligent misrepresentation, so rescission and/or damages are available.

Question 2

A private seller is attempting to sell her rare antique grandfather clock to a potential buyer. While discussing the sale of the clock, the seller states that "there is no damage to the mechanism" and that the clock will therefore accurately tell the time as long as it is regularly wound up. The seller made this statement because she had recently been told this by the restorer she paid to service the clock. After more discussion, the buyer agrees to purchase the clock for £5,000.

Two months later, a friend of the buyer who is an expert clock restorer inspects the grandfather clock and find that there is actually considerable corrosion in the mechanism, which means that the clock would not accurately tell the time. The buyer runs a business which provides furniture for use on film sets and in the background of photoshoots.

Will the contract be voidable for misrepresentation?

A. Yes, because the seller appears to have made a fraudulent misrepresentation. The statement about the mechanism may well have been actively present to the buyer's mind at the time of purchase.
B. Yes, because the seller appears to have made an innocent misrepresentation. The statement about the mechanism may well have been actively present to the buyer's mind at the time of purchase.
C. Yes, because the seller appears to have made an innocent misrepresentation. It is likely that but for the statement, the buyer would not have purchased the clock.
D. No, because the seller appears to have made a fraudulent misrepresentation. The statement about the mechanism may well have been actively present to the buyer's mind at the time of purchase.
E. No, because the seller appears to have made an innocent misrepresentation. It is likely that but for the statement, the buyer would still have purchased the clock.

10 Mistake

10.1 Chapter overview

As illustrated in the previous chapter, misrepresentation serves as an example of a vitiating factor which invalidates a contract. Mistake is another example of a vitiating factor, which if operative will invalidate a contract, rendering it void. This implies that the contract never came into existence. This chapter will consider the various categories of an operative mistake. It will consider common mistake, mutual mistake, and unilateral mistake. The chapter will focus in particular on categories of common mistake, and on unilateral mistake as it relates to identity.

10.2 What is a mistake?

A mistake often refers to a situation where the parties have entered a contract but one or both parties have made false assumptions during its formation. Therefore, it is unlikely that both parties have reached a legally enforceable agreement. The doctrine of mistake is closely linked to the discharge of a contract by frustration. Frustration occurs after the contract has been formed (a subsequent event), whereas a mistake occurs during the formation of a contract. The impact of frustration on future obligations under a contract will be further discussed in Chapter 13.

Either party can make a mistake, however, in some cases, these mistakes may invalidate the contract even though the valid elements to form a binding contract exist.[1] There are three different types of mistakes, namely common mistakes, mutual mistakes, and unilateral mistakes. These categories will be discussed in turn.

10.3 Common mistake

A common mistake is a mistake where both parties are under the same false assumption when forming a contract. In short, both parties have made the same mistake. There are three categories of mistakes under common mistakes. It is important to distinguish between them.

1 Offer, acceptance, consideration, intention to create legal relations, and capacity.

DOI: 10.4324/9781032642161-14

10.3.1 Mistake as to the existence of the subject matter: *res extincta*

In general, a mistake regarding the existence of the subject matter will render the contract void. Consider this example:

> Jade and Bill entered a contract for Bill to sell his unique wooden rare vintage cabinet worth £5,000 to Jade which had been in storage for over 3 years. The day before the contract was formed the storage company had a fire, of which Jade and Bill were not aware. The next day both parties form a contract for the sale of the unique wooden rare vintage cabinet. A few days later Bill informs Jade that the vintage cabinet had been destroyed in the fire.

Will the contract be void for mistake as to the existence of the subject matter?

It is clear that both Jade and Bill are under a mistaken belief that the subject matter is in existence and subsequently have entered into a contract based on this assumption/belief. The existence of the unique wooden rare vintage cabinet is fundamental and crucial to the contract, and without the unique wooden rare vintage cabinet the contract cannot be carried out. As the subject matter has ceased to exist before the contract was formed, there is no legal obligation for any of the parties to fulfil any contractual obligations and therefore the contract is void.[2]

10.3.2 Mistake as to title: *res sua*

In practice, this is not common. It concerns cases where a person owns the thing in question (a mistake about ownership).[3] For example, the sale of a house where the buyer already owns the property.

10.3.3 Mistake as to quality

A mistake regarding the quality of the subject matter does not invalidate a contract. This aligns with contractual principles, stating that because the parties or one party have made a bad bargain, it should not render the contract void.[4]

10.4 Mutual mistake

A mutual mistake, also known as a cross-purpose mistake, occurs when there has been a misunderstanding of both parties' intentions. It is said that both parties are at cross purposes, in other words, both parties mean something different in terms of the subject matter.[5]

2 For an example, see *Couturier v Hastie* [1856] 5 HL Cas 673. This is now confirmed in S6 Sale of Goods Act 1979.

3 *Cooper v Phibbs* [1867] LR 2 HL 149.

4 See *Bell v Lever Bros* [1932] AC 161 and *Leaf v International Galleries* [1950] 2 KB 86.

5 *Raffles v Wichelhaus* [1864] 2 Hurl & C 906.

Consider this example.

Zahira owns two similar caravans which are both white named Cara 900 Turbo. Zahira has agreed to sell Shah one of her Cara 900 Turbo caravans. One Cara 900 Turbo contains cooking facilities and a state-of-the-art entertainment system, and the other only has a microwave which has no cooking facilities. Shah thinks that he has agreed to buy the Cara 900 Turbo that contains a state-of-the-art entertainment system and cooking facilities. Zahira believes it is the other the Cara 900 Turbo without the state-of-the-art entertainment system. It is not clear which caravan they have agreed to sell, and whether Zahira is obliged to sell Shah a caravan. Has Zahira contracted to sell the Cara 900 Turbo with the state-of-the-art entertainment system?

It is clear that both parties are at cross purposes, and it cannot be decided which Cara 900 Turbo is the intended subject matter of the contract. In practice, this would be too ambiguous to enforce, and the contract would be void for mistake.

10.5 Unilateral mistake

A unilateral mistake is where one party is mistaken about something concerning the contract, and the other party is aware of the mistake[6] or deemed to be aware of the mistake. An operative unilateral mistake rendering the contract void must be a mistake as to a fundamental term of the contract.[7] Consider this scenario.

Lucas sees an advertisement on a website called TVs R Us Online Wholesalers for a 52-inch plasma TV. It is priced at £4.49 instead of £449.00. Lucas knows that the TVs should be priced at £449. Lucas places an order of ten TVs. Due to this error other customers have placed orders. TV R Us noticed an increased demand for TVs and immediately cancelled the orders, rectified the mistake; and refunded any money paid.

Is TVs R Us obliged to sell the ten 52-inch plasma TVs to Lucas and the other customers who have placed an order?

Lucas is aware that there has been a pricing error. A reasonable person would have known that there is a pricing error displayed and therefore Lucas and the other customers that placed the order will not be entitled to the TV at that price as there will not be a binding contract.[8]

6 See *Hartog v Colin & Shields* [1939] 3 All ER 566.
7 *Hartog v Colin & Shields* [1939] 3 All ER 566.
8 Note that this area also covers material studied in Chapter 1 (contract formation) in that the advertisement would amount to an invitation, and in any case, TV R Us will not have to honour the orders. Even if there is agreement through an online purchase, it is likely that terms of the contract imposed by TV R Us will allow for a mis-pricing situation.

10.5.1 Unilateral mistake as to identity

Consider the following scenario:

> Jacob owns a designer clothes store. One day, Karen visits the store. She tells Jacob that she is the famous influencer 'Kaz1234' and has millions of followers on social media. Because of the potential good publicity, Jacob agrees to let Karen film herself leaving the store with thousands of pounds worth of designer clothes. Karen tells Jacob that her assistant will then pay for the items. Karen leaves the store and her "assistant" runs away. Karen sells the clothes to Leanne for £1,500. Jacob finds out that Karen is not actually the real 'Kaz1234'. Karen and her assistant have now disappeared.

In cases of mistaken identity like the scenario above, the courts are required to apportion loss between the two innocent parties. One innocent party must suffer or bear the loss. Either:

- Jacob has a valid contract with Karen, in which case title (ownership) to the goods has passed to Karen, who has then validly passed the title on to Leanne. Leanne therefore owns the clothes, and the law will not take her property away to return the goods to Jacob; or
- Jacob's contract with Karen was void for unilateral mistake, because he was mistaken about Karen's identity. Because the contract was void, no rights passed under it, so Karen had no title to the goods to pass on to Leanne in turn. Jacob remains the legal owner of the goods so the law will return them to him.

A mistake as to identity will render the contract void in common law.[9] Where it is found that it is not, the original contract will be voidable for misrepresentation (discussed further in Chapter 9). However, this is of little help to the original seller, because in fact patterns like the scenario above, the "rogue" who obtained the goods cannot be traced to sue for damages. See Figure 10.1.

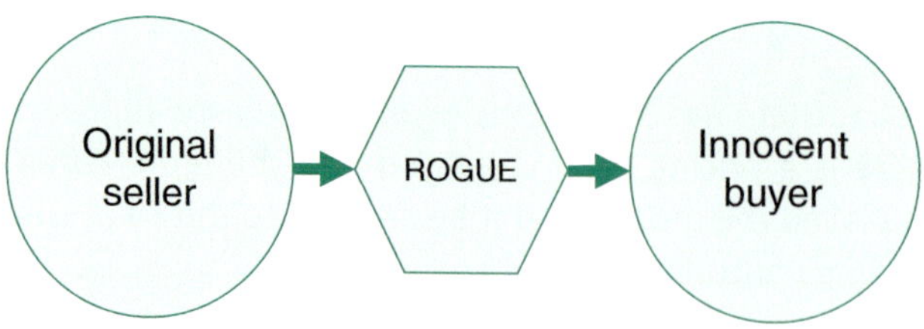

Figure 10.1 Unilateral mistake as to identity

9 See *Lewis v Averay* [1972] 1 QB 198.

For the contract to be void, the *identity* of the person must be of crucial importance to the seller (i.e. the seller only sold because the buyer was the specific person they claimed to be) and not merely their *creditworthiness* (i.e. whether the seller chose to sell because they trusted the person in front of them). In practice, this means that a contract will not be void for a unilateral mistake unless the claimant can prove that the identity of that person was crucial, and had they known this, they would not have contracted with the party.[10]

The law varies depending on whether parties are dealing face to face or at a distance, otherwise known as dealing at "arm's length".

Face-to-face transactions

In face-to-face transactions, the law stipulates that the claimant intends to deal with the person in front of them regardless of their identity. Therefore, it is for the claimant to indicate and prove that if it was not for the identity of that person, he or she would not have contracted with the other party.[11] If the person intended to deal with the person in front of them and was simply mistaken about their creditworthiness, the unilateral mistake will not be operative, and therefore the contract will not be void at common law for a unilateral mistake.

Arm's-length transactions

Where parties are not contracting face-to-face, in other words, the parties contracting are not physically present but are dealing at a distance ("arm's length"), it is assumed that the identity of the person is of crucial importance.

Where eventual buyer knows goods are stolen

Where the purchaser can prove that they bought the goods in good faith without any notice of a defective title (i.e. does not know the goods are stolen), the third party can acquire a good title, leaving the seller without any remedy unless they can demonstrate unilateral mistake. However, if the third party is aware of a defective title or should have known the title was defective, the third party (the person who purchased the goods) will always have to return the goods to the original owner.[12]

10 This is best illustrated in the House of Lords decision in *Shogun Finance v Hudson* [2004] 1 AC 919, where the courts had to apportion loss between two innocent parties. The House of Lords reaffirmed the rules relating to face-to-face transactions and transactions at a distance.

11 For an important case on unilateral mistake as to identity, see *Lewis v Averay* [1972] 1 QB 198. For other key cases see *Cundy v Lindsay* [1878] 3 App Cas 459; *Phillips v Brooks* [1919] 2 KB 243; *Ingram v Little* [1961] 1 QB 31.

12 See S23 Sale of Goods Act 1979: "When the seller of goods has a voidable title thereto, but his title has not been avoided at the time of the sale, the buyer acquires a good title to the goods, provided he buys them in good faith and without notice of the seller's defect in title."

Chapter 10 Revision Points

Mistake

- Will render a contract void
- Types of mistake:
  - Common – both parties are mistaken about the same thing
  - Mutual – both parties mistaken but about different things (facts)
  - Unilateral – only one party is mistaken, however in some cases one party takes advantage of the mistake (i.e. unilateral misstatement to identity)

It is important to check your knowledge using the following Multiple Choice Question.

Multiple Choice Question

Question 1

Aisha, a rogue, purchased a platinum ring for £8,000 from Hamish, who owns a jewellery shop in Batton Gardens. In conversation, Aisha told the seller Hamish that she was Sirianna, a famous R&B singer. Hamish responded and told her that she looked like the real Sirianna he was familiar with, the famous R&B singer. Aisha said she needed the platinum ring as soon as possible for a performance that night.

Aisha then took out an old chequebook from her bag, as she said she did not trust digital forms of payment. She wrote out a cheque in Sirianna's name. Hamish allowed Aisha to take the ring. Aisha immediately sold the ring to Oscar. Unfortunately, the cheque bounced, and the ring has been traced back to Oscar (an innocent purchaser), who now has it in his possession. Hamish now wishes to recover the ring from Oscar.

Which of the following best describes Hamish's legal position?

A. Hamish cannot void the contract because ultimately, he has made his decision based on identity. Oscar has acquired a good title to the ring. Therefore Hamish cannot get his ring back.
B. The contract will only be voidable for fraudulent misrepresentation, but not for unilateral mistakes to identity. Therefore Hamish will be able to claim his ring back.
C. Hamish can void the contract because ultimately, he has made his decision based on identity. Oscar has acquired a good title to the ring. Therefore Hamish can get his ring back.
D. Hamish cannot void the contract because ultimately, he has made his decision based on credit worthiness. Oscar has acquired a good title to the ring. Therefore, there would be a third-party right, and Hamish cannot get his ring back.
E. Hamish can void the contract because ultimately, he has made his decision based on credit worthiness. Oscar has acquired a good title to the ring. Therefore Hamish will be able to claim his ring back.

11 Duress and undue influence

11.1 Chapter overview

This chapter will outline the vitiating elements of duress and undue influence. After distinguishing between the two doctrines, the chapter will start by considering duress as a vitiating factor. It will highlight the key requirements for a claim in duress, with an emphasis on economic duress. It will explain the increasingly important distinction between unlawful and lawful act duress. The chapter will then go on to consider undue influence. After outlining the need for actual undue influence in all cases, the discussion will consider two anomalous features of undue influence: the evidential presumption in some contracts that undue influence may have taken place and the effect of undue influence by a third party on a party to a contract.

11.2 Duress and undue influence distinguished

Duress and undue influence have many similarities. Both are doctrines under which a contract will become voidable (voidable in the sense that the affected party has the choice to set the contract aside, rather than void in the sense that the contract is automatically invalid). Both, where claimed successfully, lead to the remedy of rescission (the equitable remedy which restores parties to their pre-contractual positions, discussed more fully in Chapter 9). Most importantly, both set aside contracts for the same underlying reason – that because of the pressure or coercion placed on a party entering the contract, it cannot be said that this party entered the contract willingly.[1]

The difference between the doctrines is difficult to state concisely, and there has been considerable overlap over time. Historically, duress was a creation of the common law while undue influence developed in equity. Today, the key distinction is that duress requires a specific threat or pressure from one party to the other. Undue influence recognises more subtle pressure, falling short of duress, such as where one party abuses a relationship of dominance or trust and confidence over

1 *Lynch v D.P.P. of Northern Ireland* [1975] AC 653.

DOI: 10.4324/9781032642161-15

the other. Undue influence can also apply when the influence comes from a third party, outside of the immediate contract.

In relation to both doctrines, the courts have been keen to stress that mere "hard bargaining" is not enough to vitiate a contract. As with many areas of contract law, the courts are more likely to intervene where there is a clear disparity in bargaining power, as opposed to commercial agreements negotiated between experienced businesspeople with access to legal advice.

11.3 Duress

Duress can be defined as the application of illegitimate pressure by one party to the other (or by their employee or agent), which has the effect of causing the other party to enter into the contract. Therefore, in order to establish duress, a party must first identify the illegitimate pressure they were placed under and then must show that it was this pressure which caused them to enter into the contract. The law has recognised three broad "types" of duress, categorised based on what is being threatened:

1. Duress to the person, or physical duress. This is where a party threatens physical violence or physical restraint (imprisonment).[2] The threat may be against the party themselves, someone close to them (such as a partner or family member), or their employee or agent.[3]
2. Duress to goods. This is where the threat is to destroy, damage, or seize property owned by the person being threatened.[4]
3. Economic duress. This is where the threat is not to cause physical damage to persons or property, but is to the economic interests of the other party. An example would be a threat to delay delivery of crucial raw materials needed by a business to manufacture their products.

11.3.1 Illegitimate pressure

The first requirement is that illegitimate pressure is placed on one party by the other. Note that the requirement is for the pressure to be illegitimate – not (necessarily) illegal.

Unlawful act duress

Any threat to do an unlawful act is almost certain to be found to constitute illegitimate pressure. Most obviously, this includes criminal acts – almost all cases of

2 *Barton v Armstrong* [1976] AC 104.

3 See for example *Singh v Redford* [2018] EWHC 2390 (Ch). It has been suggested that threats to a stranger or even threats of self-harm to the threatening party may be sufficient in some cases: see *Ukraine v Law Debenture Trust Corp Plc* [2023] UKSC 11.

4 *Occidental Worldwide Investment Corp v Skibs A/S Avanti* [1976] 1 Lloyd's Rep. 293.

duress to the person or to goods are threats of committing a crime. Blackmail is also a crime, so a threat to do a lawful act in revealing incriminating or embarrassing information about a party in order to force them to agree to a contract will be unlawful, even though the threatened behaviour itself is not illegal. Importantly, a threat to commit a tort or to breach a contract is also "unlawful" in this sense, and thus such a threat will usually be considered to be illegitimate pressure. What is important is that the threat is illegitimate – not that it is specifically criminal.

Lawful act duress

Traditionally, it was considered impossible for duress to arise where the threatened act was one which a party had a right to do. Consider the following scenario:

> Blimp Business Ltd has an existing contract with Crestal Climate Ltd. Under the agreement, Blimp Business buys consignments of air conditioning units every three months from Crestal Climate. One of the terms of the agreement is that the price payable for the goods is due on delivery; however, in practice Crestal Climate have informally agreed to allow Blimp Business to pay a number of months later.

Crestal Climate now wish to enter into a further contract to sell refrigerators to Blimp Business. They tell Blimp Business "if you don't enter the new contract at the price we want, we'll start demanding payment on delivery of the air conditioning units".

While it might be argued that Crestal Climate are not acting morally, they are not acting unlawfully. What they are threatening to do, enforcing the terms of an existing contract, is their lawful right. Exercising a lawful right is very unlikely to amount to economic duress.[5]

However, in recent years the courts have accepted that in some, albeit narrow, circumstances, a threat to commit a lawful act (which does not constitute the crime of blackmail) may constitute illegitimate pressure for the purpose of demonstrating duress.[6] To date, two situations have been recognised where so-called lawful act duress might arise:

1 Where the defendant uses knowledge of criminal activity by the claimant (or a close family member of the claimant) to threaten reporting the crime or initiate a private prosecution[7];
2 Where the defendant uses "reprehensible means" to force the claimant to waive an existing legal right against the defendant.[8]

5 See for example *CTN Cash and Carry Ltd v Gallaher Ltd.* [1994] 4 All ER 715.
6 *Pakistan International Airline Corp v Times Travel (UK)* Ltd [2021] UKSC 40.
7 See for example *Kaufman v Gerson* [1904] 1 KB 591.
8 See for example *Borrelli v Ting* [2010] UKPC 21.

11.3.2 Causation

The second element is a matter of causation – the illegitimate pressure must cause the party claiming duress to have entered into the contract.

Physical duress

In cases of physical duress, threat only needs to be *a* reason that the person entered the contract. It does not need to be the sole reason, or even the predominant reason. The burden of proof is on the other party to show that the threat was not in any way an influence on the threatened party's decision to enter the contract.[9]

Duress to goods and economic duress

It appears that in cases of duress to goods or of economic duress, a stricter test is applied, going beyond the threat being simply a reason to enter the contract.[10] However, this approach has not been tested beyond the High Court and even if the test does differ, it is unclear whether the appropriate test in such cases is that the threat was a "significant cause" or a "but for" test (but for the threat, the threatened party would not have entered the contract).

Evidential factors

While sometimes expressed as additional requirements, there are a number of factors which are not required to establish causation, but which, where present, can provide evidence of the impact of the threat on the defendant's behaviour. These include:

- Whether the threatened party protested at the time the contract was made;
- Whether the threatened party had access to independent legal advice;
- Whether the threatened party took prompt steps to avoid the transaction.

11.3.3 No reasonable alternative

One factor which does appear to act as a third requirement, if only in cases of economic duress, is that the claimant must show they had no reasonable alternative but to enter into the contract. In order for this to prevent a claim of economic duress (where illegitimate pressure and causation have been shown), the defendant must demonstrate that the claimant did have an alternative course of action, and this was a practical and reasonable one in the circumstances. Consider the following scenario:

> Simon is an aspiring artist who has been given the opportunity to display his paintings at an internationally famous art exhibition. He has contracted with Tomasz to transport the paintings the day before the exhibition from his studio in a remote part of North Wales to London, where the exhibition is

9 *Barton v Armstrong* [1976] AC 104.
10 *Huyton SA v Peter Cremer GmbH & Co* [1999] 1 Lloyd's Rep 620.

being held. Two hours before he is due to collect the paintings, Tomasz calls Simon and tells him "Unless you pay me double, I'm not taking the paintings".

Simon does, arguably, have alternatives. He could look for an alternative carrier. However, it is highly unlikely given the exhibition is tomorrow that Simon will be able to find an alternative carrier at such short notice, especially given his remote location. The alternative is not practical. Another option for Simon would be to let Tomasz breach the contract, and then sue. However, this exhibition is of crucial importance to Simon's career as an artist. Potentially receiving a sum of damages (which would in itself be difficult to calculate) at some future point is not a reasonable alternative to displaying his paintings at the show. In the circumstances it is very likely that if Simon agrees to pay double, the contract will be set aside for economic duress.[11]

11.3.4 Effect of duress

In the preceding scenario, it was suggested that the contract would be set aside. It is important to clarify that what would be set aside would be the "new" contract between Simon and Tomasz, under which Simon agreed to pay double. Simon would remain liable to Tomasz under the original contract at the original price (presuming Tomasz does transport the paintings) because this contract is not tainted by duress.

The way in which a contract is set aside is through the equitable remedy of rescission, which was discussed in relation to misrepresentation in Chapter 9. Rescission operates in the same way for duress, with the same potential bars which can prevent the remedy being awarded. Damages are not available as a contractual remedy for duress, but it is possible that where a threat has been made, the tort of intimidation has been committed which would allow for a monetary remedy.[12]

11.4 Undue influence

As noted above, undue influence overlaps with duress. There are many situations where both factors can apply. However, undue influence is generally considered to be broader than duress, because it focuses on the wider relationship between the parties, rather than specific threats made by one party to the other. The idea is that one party has acquired some measure of influence over the other, and has used this influence in an undue way (i.e. in a way that equity will not countenance) in order to make the other party enter into a contract.

In all cases of undue influence, the claimant must show that they were unduly influenced by another person. However, the law distinguishes between "actual"

11 See *B&S Contracts and Design v Victor Green Publications* [1984] ICR 419 on which this scenario is loosely based.

12 See *Rookes v Barnard* [1964] AC 1129 for an example of tortious damages being awarded as a result of an unlawful threat to breach a contract.

and "presumed" undue influence.[13] Technically, a claimant has the same burden of proving they were unduly influenced in all cases.[14] However, in practice there is still a distinction made between cases of "actual" undue influence, where the onus is on the claimant to prove what has occurred entirely on the evidence adduced; and "presumed" undue influence, where the circumstances of the case may mean that the court does presume undue influence has occurred and it is for the defendant to rebut that presumption.

11.4.1 Actual undue influence

In order to demonstrate actual undue influence, the evidence must show that:

- Party A had the capacity to exercise influence over Party B;
- Party A did exercise that influence;
- Party A exercised the influence unduly;
- Party A exercising the influence caused Party B to enter the transaction.

Capacity to influence

In many cases of undue influence, there will be a pre-existing relationship between the parties. However, this is not required – the parties may be encountering one another for the first time, but Party A might still have influence over Party B.

Exercise of influence

The question is whether Party A has used their influence to the extent that it has impaired Party B's free will. The court will look subjectively at the particular parties and their characteristics – so the same pressure placed on a well-informed businesswoman with access to independent legal advice may not impair her free will, but the same pressure placed on an elderly and infirm man isolated in a care home may well impair his free will.

Influence was undue

That Party A has exercised influence does not, in itself, invalidate the transaction. It must be shown that what Party A did was in some way undue, or unconscionable.[15] This may be because Party A engages in overt unacceptable behaviour, such as bullying, harassing, or dominating Party B. It may be because Party A lies to Party B, or conceals facts from them. It may be that the transaction is so clearly in favour of Party A and against the interests of Party B, that the influence must have been exercised unduly.

13 At one point these categories were also known as "Class 1" and "Class 2" undue influence, respectively, but these labels have been judicially criticised. See comments of Lord Clyde in *Royal Bank of Scotland Plc v Etridge (No.2)* [2001] UKHL 44.

14 *Royal Bank of Scotland Plc v Etridge (No.2)* [2001] UKHL 44.

15 *Daniel v Drew* [2005] EWCA Civ 507.

Causation

It must be shown that the undue influence caused the transaction, but the test is simply that the undue exercise of the influence was a reason in Party B entering the contract – it does not need to be shown that it was the sole reason, or that Party B would not have entered the contract without the influence being exercised.[16]

11.4.2 Presumed undue influence

Because undue influence is intended to combat insidious, subtle pressure, it is often extremely difficult for a claimant to adduce convincing evidence that such influence was exercised. Consider the following scenario:

> Betsy, a 97 year old woman, recently died. Her daughter, Carla, was shocked to find that before her death, Betsy agreed to sell the freehold of her house, worth £300,000 to Damon, for just £25,000. Damon is a self-styled "Guru" who runs a fringe religious organisation which Betsy joined a year before her death. Since joining Damon's organisation, Betsy rarely spoke to friends and family, spending much of her time alone with Damon.

Clearly the facts suggest that the sale of Betsy's house may have been the product of undue influence. But given Betsy has died, it will be practically impossible for Carla to provide evidence of what Damon may have said or done to persuade Betsy into the transaction.

As a result, the law has developed a presumption that undue influence is present in certain transactions. In order to rely on the presumption, the claimant must show two prerequisites:

1. There was a relationship of influence between Party A and Party B;
2. The transaction between Party A and Party B was one which "calls for explanation".

If both prerequisites can be shown, the court will presume undue influence took place, shifting the burden of proof to the defendant who must show on the balance of probabilities that there was not undue influence.

Relationship of influence

There are a number of relationships which will always be considered relationships of influence. These relationships include:

- Solicitor and client;
- Medical adviser and patient;

16 *UCB Corporate Services Ltd v Williams* [2002] EWCA Civ 555.

- Religious leader and follower;
- Trustee and beneficiary;
- Parent and child.

While parents are assumed to have a relationship of influence over their children, no other family relationships fall into this category. There is thus no rule that spouses, cohabitees, siblings etc. have relationships of influence over one another.

However, outside of the set relationships which are always considered to be ones of influence, it is open to the claimant to show on the facts that there was such a relationship. There is no single test for the court to apply in this situation, beyond deciding whether the relationship was one in which Party A had influence over Party B. However, usually such relationships will be found where Party B placed trust and confidence in Party A, or relied or depended upon Party A.

Transaction calls for explanation

It is important to remember that the first prerequisite only shows that there was a relationship of influence – not that this influence was used unduly. This is the role of the second prerequisite, where the claimant must show that the contract in question was one which "calls for explanation",[17] or "that cannot be explained by ordinary motives".[18]

The court will look objectively at the contract made at the time it was made. As such, the fact that the transaction has, because of some unforeseen event, ended up being particularly beneficial or particularly disadvantageous to one party is not relevant. Factors which might suggest a transaction calls for explanation include:

- Sale of an asset at an undervalue, or purchase for an overly high price;
- Where one party agrees to stand as surety for the debts of another;
- Where one party takes on a disproportionate level of risk given the potential benefit;
- Where the transaction involves a large portion of one party's assets.

Rebutting the presumption

The presumption is rebuttable, by evidence to the contrary. Most obviously, the defendant can provide the explanation which the transaction calls for. The other common way of rebutting the presumption is showing that the claimant had access to independent advice about the transaction (for example, from a lawyer, accountant, or independent financial adviser).

17 *Royal Bank of Scotland Plc v Etridge (No.2)* [2001] UKHL 44 per Lord Nicholls.
18 *Royal Bank of Scotland Plc v Etridge (No.2)* [2001] UKHL 44 per Lord Scott.

11.4.3 Effect of undue influence

The effect of undue influence is the same as that of duress. It makes the transaction voidable, rather than void. The party influenced may request rescission of the transaction, but this is at the court's discretion and rescission may be barred. For example, if the transaction was entered into a long time ago, the passage of time may make rescission unavailable.

11.4.4 Undue influence of a third party

One particular line of cases has considered the position where Party A enters into a contract with Party B, and Party B then claims they entered the contract due to the undue influence of Person C. In such a case, Party B may be allowed to set aside the transaction not only if Person C was acting as an agent of Party A, but also where Party A simply knew (had actual notice), *or ought to have known* (had constructive notice), of the undue influence.

Most cases relating to constructive notice have involved the same fact pattern, shown in the following scenario:

> Colin and Bao have been married for a number of years. They live together with their children in a home owned by Bao. Colin has a very domineering relationship with Bao, who relies on Colin entirely for advice about financial and legal matters. Colin wants to take out a large loan from Amazing Bank for his failing business. Colin has no assets he can use as security for the loan, so he pressures Bao into agreeing to use their family home as security. Colin's

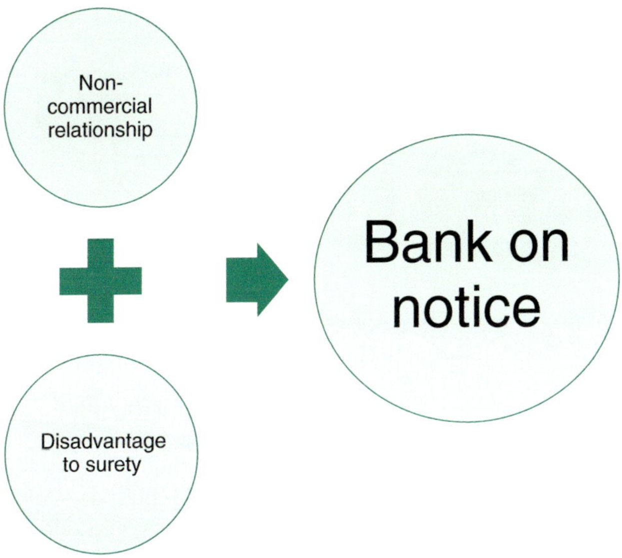

Figure 11.1 Constructive notice of undue influence

business fails and he is unable to repay the loan. Amazing Bank now seek to force sale of the family home.

Colin is not the agent of Amazing Bank, and it is highly unlikely that Amazing Bank had actual notice of the undue influence. The question becomes whether Amazing Bank had constructive notice – ought they have known that this might be a transaction "tainted" by undue influence?

Case law has established a clear set of principles which govern constructive notice in such cases. The bank will be put "on inquiry" in cases where there is a non-commercial relationship between the borrower and the surety (the person who is agreeing to be liable if the borrower does not repay the money) and the transaction is, on the face of it, to the surety's disadvantage. See Figure 11.1.

If this is the case, the bank must require the surety to take independent advice (in practice, this is almost always from a solicitor). The steps required are summarised in Figure 11.2.

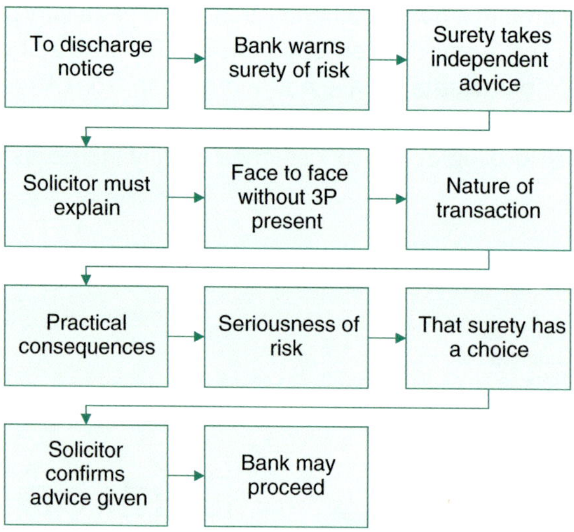

Figure 11.2 Avoiding constructive notice

Chapter 11 Revision Points

Duress

- Types
  - To person
  - To goods
  - Economic
- Requirements
  - Illegitimate pressure
  - Causation
  - No alternative (if economic)
- Effect
  - Rescission
  - Bars to rescission

Undue influence

- Actual undue influence
- Presumed undue influence
  - Established relationships
  - Or prove relationship on facts
  - Calls for explanation
  - Burden on defendant to refute
- Effect
  - Rescission
  - Bars to rescission
- Undue influence and third parties
  - When bank on notice
  - Must take steps outlined in case law

It is important to check your knowledge using the following Multiple Choice Questions.

Multiple Choice Questions

Question 1

A barber borrows £100,000 from a private lender to finance setting up a barbershop. It is agreed that the barber will repay £110,000 in one year. Five months into the agreement, the lender sends an employee to the barbershop. The employee smashes two windows and tells the barber that to avoid further "accidents", he must sign a revised contract under which the barber pays an additional £10,000 "insurance".

Is the revised contract enforceable against the barber?

A. Yes, because the lender did not personally make the threat to damage the barbershop.
B. Yes, because the barber did not protest at the time the contract was made.
C. No, because there is a presumption of undue influence in a contract between a lender and a borrower.
D. No, because there is lawful act economic duress.
E. No, because there is duress to goods.

Question 2

Two sisters live together in a flat owned by the younger sister. The elder sister approaches a bank, wishing to borrow £250,000 for use in her business. The bank require security for the loan and the elder sister indicates that her younger sister will stand as surety for the transaction, offering her flat as security for the loan. The bank manager meets with both sisters and explains the transaction, before asking the younger sister if she understands the risks. The younger sister indicates that she does and the loan is made.

The elder sister's business has gone into administration and the loan has not been repaid. The younger sister has evidence that she was unduly influenced by her elder sister into agreeing to stand as surety.

Can the bank enforce the contract against the younger sister?

A. No, the bank had constructive notice of undue influence. The bank failed to discharge this notice because the younger sister did not get independent advice without her elder sister present.
B. No, the bank had actual notice of undue influence. The transaction called for an explanation.
C. No, the bank manager in meeting with the younger sister unduly influenced her into entering into the transaction.
D. Yes, the bank did not have constructive notice of undue influence because there was not a husband and wife relationship between the borrower and the surety.
E. Yes, the bank had constructive notice of undue influence but successfully discharged their burden by giving the younger sister advice about the transaction.

12 Illegality

12.1 Chapter overview

In the context of contract law, illegality is often considered to refer to two, quite different, concepts. There is the idea of contracts which are illegal in themselves, such as a contract between a professional assassin and a client under which a promise is made to pay for the killing of another person. The law in this area is relatively simple, and this is considered in the first part of this chapter.

The second way in which the word "illegality" is used in contract law is more subtle – it refers to contracts which are not prohibited by statute, or which contravene criminal law, but contracts which are contrary to public policy. As this chapter goes on to explain, many issues traditionally considered matters of public policy have become less important as ideas of morality have changed. However, in one respect this remains a very important area of modern contract law, because under this type of illegality, contracts in restraint of trade are on the face of it void. The law relating to such contracts is the focus of the remainder of this chapter.

12.2 Contracts to commit a legal wrong

It is a well-established principle of civil law that no legal action should be permitted from a "base cause". This is encapsulated in the Latin maxim *Ex turpi causa non oritur actio*, often shortened to *Ex turpi causa* or just "illegality". Put simply, the law does not countenance a person benefiting from committing wrongdoing. As such, the usual position is that a person cannot enforce a contract to commit a crime.

However, this can be problematic in contract law because there are two parties to a contract. In contracts made for the purpose of committing a legal wrong, it is quite possible that simply refusing to enforce the contract would still lead to one of the guilty parties being (unjustly) enriched. Consider the following scenario:

> Bill is the planning officer for a local council. Clare is a property developer seeking planning permission. Clare wants to build a new housing estate in the area because the government has announced it will be building a new railway

DOI: 10.4324/9781032642161-16

link. They agree Clare will give Bill £5,000 and in exchange Bill will ensure planning permission is granted, even though Clare's proposal would normally be rejected. Just before the decision is due to be made, the government cancels the plans for the new railway. Clare sues Bill for the return of her £5,000.

A court hearing this case is in a difficult position. A decision that the contract is void and unenforceable means that Bill keeps the £5,000 – so he essentially makes a profit of £5,000 by agreeing to take a bribe and abuse his role in local government. However, a decision that Bill must return the money seems to uphold an illegal contract. Will the contract be enforceable?

12.2.1 The factors-based approach

Modern contract law has adopted an approach based on three factors.[1] When considering whether to enforce a contract to commit a legal wrong, the court must consider:

1. The underlying purpose of the prohibition (the law making this conduct illegal);
2. Any other relevant public policy on which denial of the claim may have an impact; and
3. Whether denying the claim would be a disproportionate response to the illegality.

The first two factors will be looked at from a general, societal level. What is the point of the legal provision that has been contravened? Would allowing a claim in these circumstances be harmful to the integrity of the legal system? The third factor, whether prohibiting the claim on the grounds of illegality would be disproportionate, then asks the court to look more specifically at the individual case. Under this factor, the court will consider how serious the conduct was, how central it was to the contract, and how culpable each party was. Ultimately, the court must decide whether the illegality as a whole justifies denying the claimant the legal remedy they would otherwise be entitled to claim for.

12.3 Contracts prohibited by statute

While contracts under which a party promises to do something which is prohibited (either under statute or at common law) allow for the proportional, flexible approach outlined above, some contracts are prohibited outright. Where a statute states that a particular type of contract will not be enforceable, the courts will not undermine the purpose of the statute. Historically, one famous type of contract that was expressly legislated to not be legally enforceable was gambling contracts

1 *Patel v Mirza* [2016] UKSC 42.

(for example, where a customer bets £10 on a football team to win and the bookmaker agrees to pay £20 if they do so). However, due to a change in the law, gambling contracts now can be, and often are, legally enforced.[2]

12.4 Contracts contrary to public policy

In the history of contract law, a considerable number of different circumstances have been identified that fall under the heading of contracts not being upheld on the grounds of public policy. Many of these cases have been superseded by statute – for example, contracts to bribe a public official were originally not upheld at common law on the ground of being "injurious to good government" but would today in most cases be contracts to commit the recognised crime of bribery. Other categories have become irrelevant or exceptionally rare due to changes in public ideas of morality – for example, cases which found cohabiting with a partner without being married to be immoral.

12.4.1 Contracts in restraint of trade

The main area where the courts will still regularly rely on public policy as a reason to not uphold a contract, or a term of a contract, are contracts in restraint of trade. There is not a precise legal definition of restraint of trade. Almost all contracts limit in some way a party's ability to trade with others – for example, if A contracts to sell his car to B, it prevents him from entering an agreement to sell the same car to C. However, the doctrine usually applies where a contractual obligation directly limits a party's ability to freely enter into contracts with others. Restraint of trade clauses are particularly common in two types of contract:

- Employment contracts, where an employee promises not to work for a competitor after leaving their employment;
- Contracts for the sale of a business, where the seller promises not to compete with the business they are selling.

12.4.2 Test of reasonableness

The starting point of the law is that all restraint of trade clauses are void. This presumption can be displaced by the party seeking to enforce the clause if they can show that the clause was reasonable in two distinct ways:

1 Reasonable in the interests of the parties;
2 Reasonable in the public interest.

2 S335 Gambling Act 2005.

12.4.3 Reasonable between parties

Where one party is restraining the other from freely contracting, such as in the sale of business or employment situations referred to above, this is the pre-eminent factor. The court has to decide if the clause is reasonable having regard to the legitimate interest the party relying on the clause is seeking to protect. The clause should go only so far as is necessary to protect the interest – if it is wider than needed, it is likely to be unreasonable. In contracts for the sale of a business, the legitimate interest is the "goodwill" of the existing business, i.e. its reputation among existing and potential customers. In employment contracts, it has been established that preventing another employer from utilising the skills and experience of the employee is not a legitimate interest to protect.[3] What can be protected are "trade secrets" and/or personal connections with existing customers who could be "poached" by the new business.[4]

Because the court is considering what is reasonable between the particular parties in this particular context, what is reasonable will be a matter of fact in each case. In one contract, a worldwide restriction on starting a similar business lasting a number of years may be reasonable, while in another a restriction limited to starting a competing business within just a handful of miles for a number of months might be unreasonable.

The law also takes account of the relative bargaining power of the parties. As a general rule, what is reasonable on the sale of a business will be interpreted more generously than what is reasonable to be included in an employment contract. The reasons for this are explained in Figure 12.1.

When determining whether the clause is reasonable, or too restrictive, the court will usually have regard to three dimensions of the restriction:

- Geographic area – a clause might restrict a person from working or opening a business within a certain distance of the other party;
- Duration – a clause might restrict a person from working for a competitor or opening a business for a certain amount of time after the sale or leaving the employment;
- Scope – a clause might be drafted narrowly, for example preventing a chef from working in another Korean fast food restaurant, or widely, for example preventing a teacher from working in any school, college, university, or training provider.

3 *WC Leng & Co v Andrews* [1909] 1 Ch 763.

4 See for example *Delivery Group Ltd v Yeo* [2021] EWHC 1834 (non-dealing clause) and *Littlewoods Organisation Ltd v Harris* [1977] 1 WLR 1472 (trade secret).

Figure 12.1 Different approaches to restraint of trade clauses

12.4.4 Reasonable in the public interest

As explained above, in the common situations of employment contracts and contracts for the sale of the business, the more important factor is reasonableness between the parties. The public as a whole do not have a particular interest in whether two businesses compete or in whether an employee takes trade secrets or customers to a competitor. However, the public interest does become more important in contracts where two parties agree to restrain their own trade. It is in the interests of the public for businesses to compete in the market, as this is likely to lead to lower prices.

Anti-competitive agreements are often categorised as being either "horizontal" or "vertical".

- A *horizontal* agreement is one where two or more businesses collude to avoid competition. An example might be a town with two cycle shops, where the shops agree to not sell certain bicycles below a set (overly high) price.
- A *vertical* agreement is one between the supplier of goods and acquirer of goods: for example, a manufacturer of laptops and a shop selling electronics. Such agreements might only allow the buyer to purchase from the supplier (a common example is "tie" agreements for pubs which can only purchase drinks from a single supplier) or restrict the price at which goods can be sold.

Vertical agreements are less likely to be unreasonable in the public interest, partly because they are a standard feature of a number of commercial enterprises and partly because it may make little difference to the public where goods are sourced from.

Horizontal agreements are more likely to directly affect the public, by allowing for monopolies or "cartels", which artificially control prices to the detriment of consumers. However, such matters are normally now dealt with under specific competition law, rather than the contractual doctrine of restraint of trade.

Horizontal agreements between employers which limit the ability of employees to work for others attract particular suspicion. Case law has, for example, demonstrated that it is unlikely professional sports teams can overly restrain players' rights to move to a different employer.[5] Similarly, the courts will carefully scrutinise "exclusive service" agreements which tie an individual, often a young person in a highly competitive field, into contracts with entities such as agents or publishers.[6]

12.4.5 Severance

Unless a contract is prohibited outright by statute, it is quite possible that one or more terms of the contract will be found to be illegal, but the rest of the contract is not unacceptable. The law will, in such circumstances, normally look at whether the remainder of the agreement can be "saved" (and thus enforced). To do so, the court must be able to sever the offending words or clauses from the contract. In order for severance to be ordered, and for the remainder of the contract to thus remain legally binding, three criteria must be met.[7]

1. The offending words must pass the "blue pencil" test;
2. The remaining terms must be supported by adequate consideration;
3. The character of the contract must not significantly change.

The "blue pencil" test

The blue pencil test asks the court to imagine the offending words have been crossed out (traditionally, editors used blue pencils to edit copy). The question is whether the clause continues to make sense without these words. The court is not allowed to add or modify what remains – it can only delete words.

Consider the following scenario:

> Harvey is contesting a clause in his employment contract with Igloo Images Ltd. The offending clause reads:

5 *Eastham v Newcastle United Football Club Ltd* [1964] Ch 413.
6 See for example *Proactive Sports Management v Rooney* [2011] EWCA Civ 1444 (contract for exclusive control of a young footballer's image rights) and *Schroeder Music Publishing Co Ltd v Macaulay* [1974] 1 WLR 1308 (contract for exclusive control of rights to songs written by a young songwriter).
7 *Tillman v Egon Zehnder Ltd* [2019] UKSC 32.

> On ceasing employment with Igloo Images, the employee hereby covenants not to work with any business concerned with image rights, providing any visual content to customers, or commercial photography, for a period of three months.

Imagine Harvey now wants to work with a business that provides cartoon illustrations for use in textbooks. The court might decide that the words "providing any visual content to customers" should be severed, and the clause would continue to make sense without these words.

Supported by adequate consideration

It is possible that severing all of the offending obligations might mean that one party no longer promised anything in exchange under the contract. In that case, the contract would fail for a lack of consideration so severance cannot save the contract. Chapter 3 discusses the general requirement for consideration in more detail.

Character of contract must not change

Finally, it is important that removing the offending words or terms would not be such a significant change that the contract was no longer the sort of contract that the parties had initially agreed to enter. Consider the following scenario:

> Emma, a solicitor, enters into a contract for a "Conditional Fee Agreement" (CFA) with her client Francesco. Under the contract, Emma agrees to charge a lower fee for her work on a claim being brought by Francesco in exchange for a 200% "success fee" (a fee payable to Emma if Francesco's claim is successful). It is illegal to charge a success fee over 100%. Francesco has now won his claim but states that he does not need to pay Emma for her services, because the contract is illegal. Emma argues that while the 200% success fee must be severed, this would allow the rest of the contract to take effect, giving her payment at the lower rate.

In this situation, it is unlikely that the court would order severance. The problem is that if the success fee is removed from the contract, it is no longer a CFA, where the base fee is discounted in exchange for a bonus on success, but is instead a standard retainer. This is a very different kind of fee arrangement and so the court may well find severance would make this no longer the sort of contract the parties initially agreed.[8]

8 See *Diag Human SE, Josef Stava v Volterra Fietta (a Firm)* [2023] EWCA Civ 1107 on which this scenario is based.

Chapter 12 Revision Points

Illegality

- Contract to commit a legal wrong. Look at:
  - Underlying purpose of the prohibition
  - Relevant public policy
  - Proportionality
- Contract prohibited by statute – void
- Contract in restraint of trade
  - Presumption that will be unenforceable
  - Reasonable between parties
  - Reasonable in public interest
- Severance
  - Blue pencil test
  - Must leave adequate consideration
  - Must not change character of contract

It is important to check your knowledge using the following Multiple Choice Question.

Multiple Choice Question

Question 1

An employee has recently left his employment as a sales representative for his employer. During the course of his employment, he gained a number of skills in sales and marketing. He also developed strong relationships with a number of customers of his employer.

The employee has now commenced employment with a different company, which is a competitor to his former employer. His former employer seeks to enforce a clause within his employment which purports to prevent the employee from using his sales and marketing skills and from making contact with his former employer's customers, for a period of six months.

What is the likely approach of a court to this clause?

A. The clause is on its face void. It is likely that the restriction on the employee using the skills he has developed is unreasonable. However, the restriction on making contact with former customers may be considered reasonable.
B. The clause is on its face void. It is likely that the restriction on the employee using the skills he has developed is reasonable. However, the restriction on making contact with former customers may be considered unreasonable.
C. The clause is on its face void. However, both restrictions are in the public interest and so will be considered reasonable.
D. The clause is on its face valid. It is likely that the restriction on the employee using the skills he has developed is unreasonable. However, the restriction on making contact with former customers may be considered reasonable.
E. The clause is on its face valid. It is likely that the restriction on the employee using the skills he has developed is reasonable. However, the restriction on making contact with former customers may be considered unreasonable.

PART 4

Discharge of contract

13 Discharge by frustration

13.1 Chapter overview

There are various mechanisms by which parties can be discharged from their obligations under a contract. These include frustration, performance, agreement, breach, and expiry of time or specific event. In Chapter 14 we will consider discharge by breach and expiry of time or specific event. In Chapter 15 we will consider discharge by performance. The current chapter will focus on the doctrine of frustration as a mechanism to end a contract by considering how a contract may be frustrated and the impact of the Law Reform (Frustrated Contracts) Act 1943.

13.2 What is frustration?

When it is said that a contract is frustrated, the frustrating event automatically discharges and relieves the parties from any future contractual obligations under the contract. Frustration occurs when there is an *unforeseen* event *after* the contract has been formed which renders performance of the contract *impossible, or radically different*. For the event to be an event which frustrates the contract, it *must not be the fault* of either party. The more unforeseen the event is, the more likely it is that the contract will be frustrated.[1] If the parties have made an express provision in the contract for the type of event in question, it is unlikely that it will frustrate the contract.[2]

For a contract to be frustrated, it must be radically different from what the parties had originally agreed, without either party being at fault. Frustration is unlikely to occur if a contract simply becomes more expensive or more difficult to perform.[3] The contract is said to be radically different when the nature of the contract is fundamentally different, and obligations under it, have radically changed, making it impossible to perform. Consider this scenario:

1 For a further explanation of the relationship between foreseeability and the doctrine of frustration, see the summary by Rix LJ in *Edwinton Commercial Corporation v Tsavliris Russ (Worldwide Salvage & Towage) Ltd, The Sea Angel* [2007] 2 All ER (Comm) 634.

2 Some contracts contain *force majeure* clauses that make provisions for frustrating events such as terrorism. This allocates risk in certain events. In these cases, it unlikely that the doctrine of frustration will act as a defence as risk has been allocated in the drafting of the contract.

3 See *Davis Contractors v Fareham Urban District Council* [1956] AC 696.

DOI: 10.4324/9781032642161-18

Shelly contracted with Ade to hire a hall to perform her show. Shelly invited 30 guests. Three days before the show the hall is destroyed by a fire and as a result the hall ceases to exist. Shelly can no longer use the hall for her show. In this scenario the hall no longer exists, therefore the contract is frustrated due to the impossibility of performance.[4]

13.3 In what situations will a contract be frustrated?

There are various circumstances where the law will render non-performance as a frustrating event. These circumstances will now be discussed.

13.3.1 Subject matter destroyed: impossibility

As discussed above, where the subject matter of the contract ceases to exist, the contract will be frustrated.

13.3.2 Non-availability of parties: death and illness

In cases in terms of non-availability of parties, the contract may be frustrated. This will occur, for example, if the party is dead or suffers long-term illness.[5]

13.3.3 Non-occurrence of an event which acts as the foundation of the contract and can no longer be performed

Frustration will occur in cases where the common and only purpose of the contract is no longer possible to perform. Where this is the case, it is crucial that the purpose of the contract is the same for both parties. Two cases with different outcomes relating to the same cancelled event neatly demonstrate this rule. When the coronation of King Edward VII was postponed, a number of claims for frustration were brought. The courts held that a contract to hire a room for the sole purpose of watching the King's procession was frustrated because the common foundation and purpose of the contract had been frustrated.[6]

However, where a steamboat was hired out to the defendant "for the purpose of viewing the Naval Review and for a day's cruise round the fleet", plus the coronation celebrations, the court held that because the cruise could still go ahead, it meant that the pleasure of the trip could still be enjoyed and, therefore, there were elements of the contract that could still be performed and enjoyed.[7] It was held that the nature of the contract was not something radically different from the original contract and, therefore, did not frustrate it.

4 See *Taylor v Caldwell* [1863] 3 B & S 826.

5 See *Condor v Barron Knights Ltd* [1966] 1 WLR 87 for an example of when this may occur in terms of long term illness.

6 *Krell v Henry* [1903] 2 KB 740.

7 *Herne Bay Steamboat Co Ltd v Hutton* [1903] 2 KB 683.

13.3.4 Supervening illegality

A contract is frustrated if performing the contract becomes illegal after the parties had contracted. This may happen where the law is changed, for example a contract to supply goods to a party based in a nation that declares war.[8]

13.4 Self-induced frustration

A deliberate act, fault, or choice by either one of the parties will not give rise to frustration, although it is debatable whether a negligent act can amount to a frustrating event.[9] The burden of proof is on the party claiming self-induced frustration to prove it. If it is found that frustration is self-induced, the party who is at fault may well be in breach of their contractual obligations and, therefore, a potential claim for breach of contract may arise.

13.5 Frustration of leases

The law in terms of frustration in this area is unclear. However, the guiding legal principle when it comes to the question as to whether a lease can be frustrated is that it is extremely rare, although it is possible.[10]

13.6 Effects of frustration

A frustrating event in practice will mean that it has become impossible for both parties to perform their obligations as expected.[11] This can lead to an unfair situation where one party has already performed. For example, if one party had paid the full sum and the frustrating event was no fault of either party, and that party was not able to claim the money back, this would be unjust.

Consider this example:

> Imagine you paid over £30,000 to hire a hall for your wedding reception. The week before your wedding, a fire burns down the hall. However, the party you contracted with refused to refund your money or provide you with any compensation. It would be unfair and unjust if you were unable to recoup that money as nothing had been performed and you would be out of pocket.

The *Law Reform (Frustrated Contracts) Act 1943* has addressed the question of frustration by allowing money to be recouped in certain situations.[12] It has also clarified the consequences of a frustrating event. See Table 13.1.

8 *The Fibrosa* [1942] 2 All ER 122.
9 See *Joseph Constantine Steamship Line Ltd v Imperial Smelting Corp. Ltd* [1942] AC 154.
10 See *National Carriers v Panalpina (Northern) Ltd* [1981] 1 All ER 161.
11 *The Fibrosa* [1942] 2 All ER 122.
12 Applies only to certain types of contracts. S2(5) The Law Reform (Frustrated Contracts) Act 1943.

Table 13.1 Effect of Law Reform (Frustrated Contracts) Act 1943

Situation	Effect of the Law Reform (Frustrated Contracts) Act 1943
Money paid in advance or an agreement to make an advanced payment	Recoverable (S1(2))
Outstanding money payable or due on completion by a certain date	Money is no longer due (S1(2))
Where a party has started to perform and there are expenses incurred which have left a party out of pocket	The court can order a just sum to be paid (S1(2)) – power is discretionary, which is broad.
If it is found that a party has gained a valuable benefit	The court can order a just sum to be paid (S1(2)) taking all the circumstances of the case into account (S1(3))
Parties that have inserted provisions (a *force majeure* clause) in the contract for dealing with the consequences of frustration	Possible to exclude the Act (S2(5))

Chapter 13 Revision Points

Different ways a contract can be frustrated:

- Impossibility
- Death and illness
- Non-occurrence of an event which acts as the foundation of the contract
- Illegality
- Self-induced frustration
- Frustration of leases

Means of remedying frustration

- Common law
- Law Reform (Frustrated Contracts) Act 1943

It is important to check your knowledge using the Multiple Choice Questions below.

Multiple Choice Questions

Question 1

Spa R Us is offering a luxury bank holiday weekend break special in Yorkshire, which includes fully inclusive accommodation at a 5-star hotel, a city tour, and three hours of yoga. The evening entertainment includes a well-known soul singer, Jados Glige, and tickets to the theatre to see a well-known play starring a famous actor, Sir Dion Tichy. The booking requires full payment before the deadline. Tanika and Tyrone book two places and fully pay £800 for their tickets. Unfortunately, Sir Dion Tichy falls ill on the day, and therefore the play is cancelled.

Which of the following is the correct advice to give Tanika and Tyrone?

A. The absence of Sir Dion Tichy is one element of the package being absent, which renders the contract frustrated as the entire purpose of the contract is frustrated. Therefore, the parties will be discharged from any future contractual obligations.

B. The absence of Sir Dion Tichy is one element of the package being absent and does not give rise to frustration to the foundation of the contract. Therefore, the contract is binding on both parties.

C. Part of the contract will be frustrated; therefore, the defence will only work in terms of Sir Dion Tichy's absence. The parties will still need to fulfil their future obligations.

D. The absence of Sir Dion Tichy, one element of the package being absent, does not give rise to frustration to render the entire purpose of the contract frustrated. However, the parties can choose whether to frustrate the contract or affirm it.

E. The cancellation of the play is irrelevant to the purpose of the contract as a whole, so the contract has been completely performed and there is no claim for Tanika and Tyrone.

Question 2

Ashana and Mark have hired a hall for their wedding reception at the end of June. They have invited 300 guests from around the world. However, a week before the wedding, there is a flood, which means that the hall can no longer be used for their reception.

Which of the following best describes the legal position?

A. The contract has been frustrated because performance has been made impossible by the flooding, as the contract is radically different from what the parties had in contemplation when forming the contract. It is likely to find that the contract has been frustrated between the owners of the hall and the organisers.
B. The contract has not been frustrated, as it is not radically different from what the parties had in contemplation when forming the contract. It is likely to find that the contract has been frustrated between the owners of the hall and the organisers.
C. The contract has been frustrated because performance has been made impossible by the flooding, as the contract is radically different from what the parties had in contemplation when forming the contract. It is unlikely to find that the contract has been frustrated between the owners of the hall and the organisers.
D. The contract is radically different from what the parties had in contemplation at the time of formation. It is likely to find that the contract has been frustrated between the owners of the hall and the organisers.
E. The contract is not radically different from what the parties had in contemplation at the formation of the contract. It is likely to find that the contract has not been frustrated between the owners of the hall and the organisers.

14 Discharge by agreement, breach, or expiry of time or other specified event

14.1 Chapter overview

This chapter will begin by explaining how a contract can be ended by agreement. In particular, it will consider this in the context of forming a new contract. It will then consider the impact of breach of contract in terms of repudiation where the innocent party is relieved from any future obligations under the contract. It will also consider anticipatory breach and the right of election for the non-breaching party. The chapter will then end by looking at the discharge of a contract due to the terms contained therein.

14.2 Agreement

In some cases, parties may expressly agree to release each other from any obligations under the contract. They may also implicitly agree (through conduct) to release each other. In these circumstances, both parties agree to release each other from future obligations. Generally, under the contract, consideration is needed to discharge contractual obligations.

14.3 Breach

Where a contract has been breached, the innocent party is entitled to claim damages; in other words, a sum of money awarded for a breach to put the innocent party back in the position they would have been in had the breach not occurred.[1] As to whether the innocent party can terminate the contract (a "repudiatory breach"), this will depend on the seriousness of the breach, as discussed in Chapter 5.

14.3.1 Consequences of a repudiatory breach

Only in circumstances where the term is classified as a condition, or breach of an innominate term has led to sufficiently severe consequences, will breach amount to a repudiatory breach. Where the contract sets out circumstances in cases that this may occur or where it is concluded that the term is a condition or an innominate term, the innocent party will have the right of election or, in other words, a choice, which will entitle the innocent party to affirm the contract. This means that the

1 See Chapter 16.

DOI: 10.4324/9781032642161-19

remaining contractual obligations remain in place which both parties have to continue to adhere to or the contract comes to an end immediately. The parties are not restored to their original position as would be the case with rescission.

14.3.2 Anticipatory breach

In some situations, a party will inform the other party, in advance, that they are not willing to perform their future contractual obligations before the due date of performance. This is known as an anticipatory breach.[2] The innocent party has a choice in these circumstances to affirm[3] or discharge the contract, meaning that the parties are discharged from any future contractual obligations. The "innocent" party must be careful when choosing to treat the contract as at an end – if it later transpires the breached term was only a warranty, or innominate and the consequences of breach were minor, then the party purporting to terminate the contract could themselves be in breach by not continuing to perform.

14.4 Expiry of time or other specified event

Take, for example, you agreed to supply ready-made meals to a company for a certain time and a date was agreed between you and the other party that this arrangement would be renewed based on a six-monthly review. This would allow you to contractually supply the ready-made meals until you and the supplier reviewed the agreement once the six-month period was over. Provided these provisions are drafted in the contract, the expiry of the time will terminate the contract and release the parties from any future obligations. In other cases, a specified event outlined in a contract could bring a contract to an end. An example of a specified event could be the lockdown during the coronavirus pandemic, where many suppliers agreed to supply services or products to the NHS during that period. Once the lockdown ended, many suppliers withdrew their services. This is an example of a specific event that could bring a contractual obligation to an end, provided it had been drafted in the contract.

Chapter 14 Revision Points

A contract can end in various ways:

- Agreement
- Breach
- Expiry of time or other specified event

It is important to check your knowledge using the following Multiple Choice Question.

2 *Hochster v De la Tour* [1853] 2 E&B 678.

3 Although there are limitations on this; see *Hounslow London Borough Council v Twickenham Garden Developments Ltd* [1970] 3 WLR 538. See also *White & Carter (councils) Ltd v McGregor* [1962] AC 413.

Multiple Choice Question

Question 1

In January, Bill contracts with Carlos, a carpenter, to renovate his kitchen and build an extension in April to be ready for the summer season, as he has a special occasion, his dad's 80th birthday party. Carlos agrees to start the renovation work on 3 April. On 24 March, Bill informs Carlos by email and text message that he no longer wants him to complete the work.

What is the best advice to give Carlos?

A. This will amount to an anticipatory breach, as Bill has informed Carlos before the due date of performance that he will not perform. This anticipatory breach is repudiatory in nature as the breach goes to the root of the contract, which deprives the innocent party of substantially the whole benefit of the contract. Carlos will not be able to elect to discharge the contract and claim damages from 24 March.

B. This will amount to an anticipatory breach, as Bill has informed Carlos before the due date of performance that he will not perform. This anticipatory breach is repudiatory in nature as the breach goes to the root of the contract, which deprives the innocent party of substantially the whole benefit of the contract. Carlos will be able to elect to discharge the contract and claim damages from 24 March.

C. This will not amount to an anticipatory breach, as Bill has breached the contract by informing Carlos before the due date of performance that he will not perform. This will be a breach of the condition that allows Carlos to sue for damages and terminate the contract.

D. This will not amount to an anticipatory breach, as Bill has breached the contract by informing Carlos before the due date of performance that he will not perform. This will be a breach of a warranty, which allows Carlos to sue for damages and terminate the contract.

E. This will not amount to an anticipatory breach, as Bill has breached the contract by informing Carlos before the due date of performance that he will not perform. This will be a breach of a condition that only allows Carlos to sue for damages.

15 Discharge by performance

15.1 Chapter overview

This chapter will consider discharge by performance. It will consider the exceptions to the complete performance rule and the impact this has on contractual obligations and the ending of a contract. There are exceptions to this rule, by which the law has attempted to address its unfairness. These exceptions enable a party to claim some money for work carried out. The chapter will also briefly discuss the harshness of the rule.

15.2 Performance must be precise and exact

The general view of performance is that it must be "precise and exact", otherwise known as a complete performance. This rule does not benefit parties that have performed only part of the contract. In practice, this means that the person promising to perform must perform exactly what has been agreed in the contract. Any deviation from what has been agreed between the parties will not amount to complete performance and, therefore, the person carrying out any work will not be entitled to any payment.[1] This rule is harsh and can leave defendants with no payment for the work carried out.[2]

Consider this example:

> You are contracted to decorate a large room for the cost of £500 for Kalpesh. You start the work and complete most of the work to a high standard; but you forget to paint the back of the door. Kalpesh refuses to pay you any of the £500 because the back of the door has not been painted. The complete performance rule will mean that you will not be entitled to any money as you have not fully

1 See *Cutter v Powell* [1796] 6 Term Reports 320, where it was held that the widow could not recover a proportion of the money because her deceased husband died at sea before he completed the journey from Jamaica to Liverpool and, therefore, the contract was not fully performed. See also *Re Moore & Co's Landauer & Co's Arbitration* [1921] 2 KB 519 for another example.

2 There is also an exception in S15A under the Sale of Goods Act 1979 where, in business-to-business transactions, a slight breach will be treated as a warranty if it would be unreasonable for the buyer to reject the goods.

DOI: 10.4324/9781032642161-20

performed the contract; in other words, the performance is not "precise and exact". Because of this harsh rule, the law has developed exceptions to it to enable a performing party to recover some money for the work they have carried out.

15.3 Exceptions to the rule

While the general rule as outlined above is that performance must be precise and exact, case law has developed a number of exceptions to the rule. These are visualised in Figure 15.1 and then explained in the next sections.

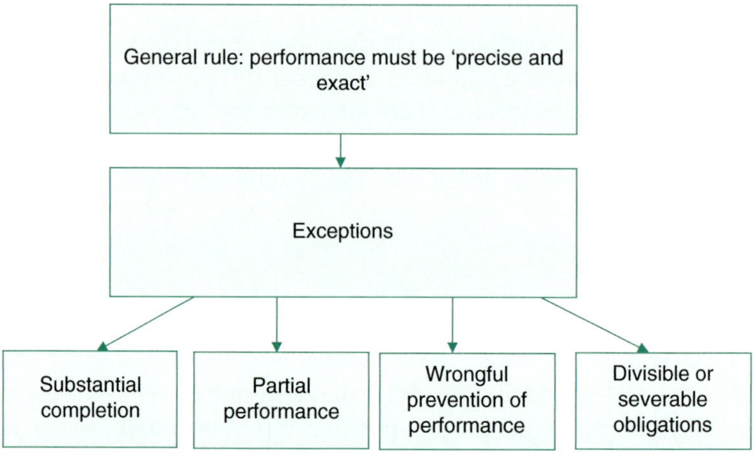

Figure 15.1 Exact performance and exceptions to the rule

15.3.1 Substantial performance

Where a party substantially performs their part of the contract, they will be entitled to the full contract price minus the amount it would cost to remedy the defective or incomplete performance.[3]

Applying this to the example above would mean that you have substantially performed, and, therefore, you will be entitled to the £500 minus the amount it would cost to remedy the defective performance. If the cost of an additional £100 for someone else to do the work you missed, you will be entitled to the £500 minus £100; i.e., the incomplete part of the contract or performance and the amount it would cost to engage a decorator to finish painting the back of the door. Kalpesh would have to pay you £400 as you had substantially performed the contract.

3 See *H. Dakin & Co Ltd v Lee* [1916] 1 KB 566.

15.3.2 Partial performance

If the obligations under a contract have not been substantially performed – in other words, there has been substantial performance – the performing party will get the total contract price minus some money set off for defects. With partial performance there is some attempt to perform but to a poor standard (not good enough) and therefore a breach. In these circumstances, a small award at the discretion of the court will be awarded to the person carrying out the performance to avoid unjust enrichment. This award is referred to as a payment on a *quantum meruit* basis, a reasonable sum for the work carried out.[4] However, to receive this payment, the person not at fault must have a genuine choice to accept partial performance.

Using the example above, imagine the paint starts to peel. In other words, your work is of poor quality or substandard. This is very likely to amount to partial performance as the work carried out is poor. Therefore, you would be entitled to a payment from Kalpesh on a *quantum meruit* basis: a reasonable sum for the work carried out or, in other words, an amount the performing party deserves. However, it is key that Kalpesh has a genuine choice to accept partial performance; that is, a voluntary acceptance of partial performance.

15.3.3 Wrongful prevention of performance

Where the performing party is willing to perform their part of the contract and they have been wrongfully prevented from performing their contractual obligation, they will be discharged from any future obligations under the contract and will be entitled to damages for breach of contract or a reasonable sum (on a *quantum meruit* basis) for the work that has already been completed under the contract.[5] Consider the scenario below:

> Oscar contracts with Jordan, a landscape gardener, to lay new paving in Oscar's garden. Jordan starts the work but has not finished. On the dates agreed with Oscar to finish the work, the gates are locked as Oscar decides to go on a cruise for a month and forgets to leave the key to enable access to the garden. In this situation, Jordan would be discharged from any future contractual obligations and would be entitled to payment for the work carried out before Jordan was prevented from laying the pavement.

15.3.4 Divisible or severable obligations

Another exception to the general rule in terms of performance being precise and exact is where the contract can be divided into severable obligations instead of a single obligation. This, sometimes referred to as entire and divisible contracts, is

4 See *Sumpter v Hedges* [1898] 1 QB 673.
5 See *Planche v Colburn* [1831] 8 Bing 14 for an example of this.

based on the intention of both parties. For example, imagine Aisha is contracted to decorate all of the flats owned by a landlord within a block of flats. On the completion of each flat, Aisha is paid a sum of money. This would be a severable contract in that Aisha will be paid at various stages during its completion.

Chapter 15 Revision Points

Discharge of contract by performance

- Performance must be precise and exact
- Exceptions
  - Substantial performance
  - Partial performance
  - Wrongful prevention of performance
  - Divisible contracts
- Time being of the essence may be used as a condition in a contract

It is important to check your knowledge using the following Multiple Choice Question.

Multiple Choice Question

Question 1

Bathroom R Us has agreed to install a new bathroom in Zahra's house, which includes tiling the walls and floor. They start the work and install the units and toilet. They tile the walls and finish tiling the floor but forget to add grout to the edges of the tiles. It has been four weeks since Zahra has seen any of the carpenters from Bathroom R Us. Zahra has called and emailed the lead carpenter to no avail and has decided not to pay the builders, as she has found another local carpenter to finish the work. It is now seven weeks since they started the work, and Bathroom R Us have now contacted Zahra to say they are willing to come back and finish the work. They demand the full contract price. Barbara refuses to pay them anything.

Which of the following statements are correct in terms of performance?

A. Bathroom R Us have substantially performed by finishing most of the work. The defects are minor, and therefore they should at least be entitled to the full contract price minus the defects.
B. Bathroom R Us have partially performed by finishing most of the work. The defects are minor, and therefore they should at least be entitled to the full contract price minus the defects.
C. Bathroom R Us have performed completely by finishing most of the work. The defects are minor, and therefore they should be entitled to the full contract price minus the defects.
D. Bathroom R Us have substantially performed by finishing most of the work. The defects are irrelevant, as it was Zahra's own choice to engage another tiler; therefore, they should at least be entitled to the full contract price.
E. Bathroom R Us have partially performed by finishing most of the work. The defects are minor, and therefore they should at least be entitled to the full contract price minus the defects.

PART 5

Remedies

16 Damages

16.1 Chapter overview

The final set of chapters considers the remedies available to the innocent party who succeeds in a claim for breach of contract. It should be remembered that other remedies are sometimes available in contract law: for example, in Chapter 9 you considered the remedy of rescission which is often used when a contract is made voidable due to the presence of a vitiating factor such as misrepresentation. However, when a contract is breached outright, the usual remedy is financial compensation in the form of damages. Because damages are such an important contractual remedy, the topic is considered over this chapter and the next chapter. This chapter will consider the different bases for calculating the amount of damages. It will begin by considering the usual expectation-based measure of damages, before going on to discuss alternative measures such as cost of cure, loss of amenity, loss of a chance, and reliance loss. Finally, the chapter will examine liquidated sums and penalties, guarantees, and indemnities.

16.2 Expectation loss

The usual measure of damages awarded in contract law is said to be expectation based. This means that the innocent party is awarded the amount of damages required to place them in the position they could have expected to be in had the contract been performed properly.[1] As such, contractual damages look "forwards" – they are not about restoring a party to a previous position, they are about placing a party in the position they should have been in had the breach not occurred.

Consider the following problem scenario:

> Stefan has contracted with Tanisha to buy Tanisha's car, a 2017 Super Speedster. They agree Stefan will buy the car for £5,000. After the contract is made, Tanisha fails to deliver the car as agreed because she has sold it to someone else who offered more. A 2017 Super Speedster in similar condition would usually cost £7,000 on the open market.

1 *Robinson v Harman* (1848) 1 Ex. 850.

DOI: 10.4324/9781032642161-22

Because contractual damages look forwards, the court must look at the position Stefan expected to be in. Stefan expected to have a 2017 Super Speedster and in order to purchase one elsewhere, he needs £7,000. He currently has £5,000 that he would otherwise have given to Tanisha. Therefore, his expectation loss is £2,000 – the £7,000 cost to buy the car elsewhere, minus the £5,000 Stefan no longer needs to pay to Tanisha.

16.2.1 The difference in value approach

The example of Stefan shows the way the law will usually take the "difference in value" approach. Damages are calculated based on the difference between what was promised and what was actually delivered. This is usually simple to calculate where the innocent party has not received goods or services promised and there is an available market for the goods or services in question. The court simply needs to take the "market price" for the goods or services in question, subtract the amount the buyer was originally going to pay, and award the outstanding amount in damages to the claimant. This approach will be taken in business to business contracts covered by the Sale of Goods Act 1979.[2] Of course, if the goods or services cost the same or less than the buyer had promised to pay, their expectation loss is nil and so no damages will be due.

The approach is more difficult when the innocent party is the one providing goods or services to the party in breach of contract: for example, where a seller, A, agrees to sell a bicycle to a buyer, B, who then refuses to accept the item. Again, the starting point is the market price where there is an available market. This approach will be taken in business-to-business contracts covered by the Sale of Goods Act 1979.[3] If the market price is lower than the price the seller had agreed, the seller will be entitled to the difference between the prices. If the market price is the same or higher, the party in breach is likely to argue that there has been no loss – so in the example, the seller could sell the bicycle to someone else, C, for at least the same amount of money.

However, what if the seller is a manufacturer of bicycles and argues that it could have sold one bicycle to B and another bicycle to C? This is known as the "lost volume" problem. The law deals with that problem by looking at the market as a whole. If supply is greater than demand, i.e. the seller could have sold the goods or services under the contract and also provided the same goods or services to another buyer, then they may claim the lost sale. If demand is greater than supply, so the seller could only have provided the goods or services to one party, not both simultaneously, then there will be no claim for lost profit.[4]

2 S51 Sale of Goods Act 1979. This provision is not mirrored in the Consumer Rights Act 2015 because this has its own set of remedies, as discussed in Chapter 6.

3 S50 Sale of Goods Act 1979.

4 *Charter v Sullivan* [1957] 2 WLR 528.

All of the above only applies when there is an available market, so the court can determine the "market price". When there is no available market, the court will need to make its own estimation of the actual value of the goods or services in question, based on the evidence before it, including the cost of the nearest equivalent.[5]

16.2.2 The cost of cure approach

An alternative way of measuring the expectation loss of the claimant is to consider the cost of curing the defective performance: in other words, the cost of making good what has been provided so that the claimant ends up with what was originally promised. Where performance has not taken place, the cost of cure approach leads to the same sum as the difference in value approach: the cost of curing Tanisha's defective performance in the earlier example is £2,000, as that is the amount needed for Stefan to end up with a sufficiently similar car to the one she was selling.

However, the cost of cure approach is of particular value when the innocent party has received some part of the goods or services but performance is defective. A common example is in contracts for building work.

Consider the following scenario:

> Harriet, a builder, has agreed to construct a conservatory for Jagpaul. The parties agree a price of £20,000 for the work. Harriet builds the conservatory, but in breach of contract her work is defective, meaning that the conservatory leaks significantly when it rains. Jagpaul spends £2,500 employing Kevin, another builder, to repair the conservatory.

It would be very difficult to take the difference in value approach, because it is hard to put a value on a defective conservatory. Instead, the logical measure of damages is the cost of cure: it has cost an additional £2,500 than originally agreed for Jagpaul to get the conservatory he contracted for, so Harriet should pay Jagpaul £2,500 in damages.

However, the cost of cure can often be very high, sometimes higher than the value of the initial performance.

Consider the following scenario:

> Martha contracts to have her house redecorated by Nish, a local decorator. They agree a cost of £2,000 for the work. Martha specifies in the contract that she wants all of the walls in the house to be painted in "Extra White", a particular shade of white paint. In breach of the contract, Nish paints all of the walls in "Pure White", a slightly different shade. The painting is otherwise

5 *Hughes v Pendragon Sabre Limited T/A Porsche Centre Bolton* [2016] EWCA Civ 18.

done to an excellent standard. It would cost £8,000 to remove the paint and repaint the walls with Extra White paint.

In this instance, the court would be very reluctant to award the full cost of cure of £8,000. This is four times the amount of money Nish contracted for. It might also be questioned whether Martha would use the £8,000 to repaint the walls, given they are already a very similar shade of white. Case law makes it clear that cost of cure damages will not be recoverable where either:

1 The cost of cure is out of all proportion to the advantage to be gained by the claimant by doing so; or
2 The claimant does not subjectively have a sufficient intention to have the repair work carried out if he or she receives damages on this basis.

Both of these concepts are aspects of the basic inquiry the court is making when asked to award cost of cure damages, rather than damages based on the difference in value: is it reasonable for the claimant to insist on having the curative work done?

16.2.3 Loss of amenity damages

Returning to Martha's scenario, what will the position be if the court declines to award the £8,000 cost of cure damages? Usually, the court would return to calculating damages based on the difference in value. But in Martha's case, it is very unlikely there is any difference in value at all. The value of her house may well be affected by whether it has been redecorated, but it is very unlikely that the value will change because the walls have been painted Pure White rather than Extra White. So under this measure of damages, Martha would receive nothing, despite the fact that Nish has clearly breached the contract and she has not got what she contracted for.

Martha's interest in getting what she bargained for is sometimes referred to as "the consumer surplus" or "the claimant's non-financial interest in performance". In certain cases, the court has recognised that the claimant has a particular interest in getting exactly what they contracted for, but that this interest cannot be easily or proportionately assessed using the cost of cure or difference in value approaches.

In such cases, the court may award "loss of amenity" damages. Loss of amenity damages represent a financial sum, set at the discretion of the court, to represent the loss of some desirable or useful thing that the claimant expected.[6] Loss of amenity is also the basis on which damages can be claimed for physical inconvenience and discomfort. It is also the basis on which damages for mental distress and disappointment can be awarded, but as you learned in Chapter 4 such damages

6 See for example *Ruxley Electronics and Construction Ltd v Forsyth* [1996] AC 344.

are only available where the contract that has been breached was one made for entertainment or enjoyment.[7]

It is important to note that the court will decide the method of calculating damages – the claimant does not choose which measure will be used.[8]

16.2.4 Loss of a chance

Sometimes, a breach of contract leads to a "speculative" loss: the loss of a chance (rather than a certainty) of gaining some benefit.

Consider the following scenario:

> Bertrand is a sculptor who creates sculptures out of rare metals. He contracts with Cadwaller and Co to purchase raw materials for a new sculpture which he wants to enter into a national art competition. In breach of contract, Cadwaller and Co deliver the materials late, which means Bertrand is unable to complete the sculpture in time to enter the competition. The competition had 9 entrants with a top prize of £20,000.

Bertrand has certainly lost something as a result of Cadwaller and Co's defective performance, but he has not necessarily lost £20,000. There were nine other entrants in the competition, so had Bertrand been able to enter he would have been in competition with these other entrants. What Bertrand has lost is a chance of winning the £20,000.

In such cases, the courts have been willing to award damages calculated by reference to the likelihood the claimant would have received the possible benefit.[9] In Bertrand's case, a common sense approach might be to consider the prize he could have won, £20,000, and his basic odds of winning (1 in 10). As such, a reasonable award might be 1/10th of the prize, i.e. £2,000.

In order to claim damages for loss of a chance, the claimant must be able to show there was a real or tangible chance that was lost. So if Bertrand had instead been prevented from buying a national lottery ticket by the defendant's breach, it would be very unlikely he would be able to claim for loss of the extremely small and speculative chance of winning the jackpot (a 1 in 45 million chance).

16.3 Reliance loss

While all of the above methods of calculating damages are ways of quantifying the claimant's expectation loss, it is also possible in some cases to claim for

7 *Farley v Skinner (No 2)* [2001] UKHL 49.
8 *Morris-Garner v One Step Forward* [2018] UKSC 20.
9 See for example *Chaplin v Hicks* [1911] 2 KB 786.

damages on a reliance basis. This means that rather than seeking compensation to put the non-breaching party in the position they would have been in had the contract been performed properly, the claimant instead seeks compensation for wasted expenditure made in reliance on the contract.

Consider the following scenario:

> Xiaoyu is a computer game developer who wants to make a computer game based on the popular "Contract Man" superhero. Xiaoyu contracts with Youssef, the owner of the intellectual property rights to Contract Man in order to use the character in his proposed game. After six months of developing the game, at a cost of £500,000, Youssef withdraws his consent for Xiaoyu to use Contract Man, in breach of their original agreement.

Proceeding on the usual basis of expectation loss, Xiaoyu would want to claim the overall loss of net profit from the potential Contract Man computer game (i.e. the amount he made from selling the game, minus the cost of developing the game). This would put him in the position he expected to be in as a result of the contract, in other words his expectation loss. However, how could the court estimate how much profit the game might have made? This would be pure speculation, as the game could have been a huge success or a catastrophic failure, or anything in between.

In situations like this one, where there is insufficient evidence to look forwards at what the result of the contract might have been or where the amount is speculative, the court can instead look backward at the loss suffered by the innocent party in reliance on the contract.[10] In Xiaoyu's case, the reliance loss is clear – it is the £500,000 spent developing the game up to the point Youssef withdrew from the contract. Of course, it may well be that not all of this expenditure was wasted, because Xiaoyu may be able to develop and sell a functioning computer game that simply does not use the intellectual property in question. This shows the limitations of a claim in reliance loss – the claimant may only claim for losses which are truly wasted in reliance on the contract. The claimant is as always expected to mitigate their losses which is explored further in Chapter 17.

16.4 Liquidated damages

Most claims for breach of contract are claims for unliquidated damages. "Unliquidated" simply means that the amount being claimed was not agreed between the parties in advance; instead, the amount of damages will be decided and calculated by the court. However, in many contracts, particularly commercial contracts, the parties will agree in advance on the amount of compensation to be paid for breach

10 See for example *Anglia Television v Reed* [1972] 1 QB 60.

of a particular term. A simple example might be in a contract for the supply of goods, where the parties agree in advance the sum the supplier must pay if they deliver the goods late.

Contract law accepts that the parties may well agree damages in advance and so it is perfectly possible for parties to include and rely on a liquidated damages clause in their contract. Such a clause, if valid, will take effect despite the true loss – so if the actual loss suffered by the innocent party is higher or lower than the amount provided for in the clause, this will not be reflected in the amount paid.

However, because such clauses can lead to a party either paying much more or much less than the true loss suffered, and because contracts are often made between parties with unequal bargaining power, the courts do look carefully at liquidated damages clauses. In some ways this is a similar approach to exemption clauses, which were discussed in Chapter 8: the courts will allow such clauses in principle but will be very alert for any possible unfairness caused by a particular clause in practice.

The courts therefore distinguish between "liquidated damages clauses" and "penalty clauses". Both phrases refer to a clause that purports to agree a sum of damages payable in the event of breach, but the key distinction is that liquidated damages clauses are valid and will be upheld, while penalty clauses are invalid and will be unenforceable. This then begs the question, what is the test to distinguish between them?

The modern test, as set out by the Supreme Court,[11] is that the party seeking to enforce the clause must show two things:

1 That they had a legitimate interest in ensuring performance of the particular obligation by the other party; and
2 That the sum payable under the clause is not extravagant or unconscionable in comparison to that interest.

16.4.1 Legitimate interest

What constitutes a legitimate interest that a party is seeking to protect will be a question of fact in each case. What is clear from the case law on the topic is that this is a wide test that does not just consider a party's narrow financial or commercial interests. For example, a company operating a car park had a legitimate interest in imposing a fine on customers who outstayed the period of free parking.[12] Commercially speaking, the company did not make any financial gain if a particular parking space continued to be occupied by person A, in comparison to the situation where

11 *Cavendish Square Holding v Makdessi; ParkingEye v Beavis* [2015] UKSC 67.
12 *Cavendish Square Holding v Makdessi; ParkingEye v Beavis* [2015] UKSC 67.

person A left on time and person B used the free parking space instead. However, the company still had a legitimate interest in protecting the overall system by which the car park was run, where people did not leave their cars longer than they had paid for. The company was looking to deter people from breaking the rules imposed for the benefit of everyone, so that parking spaces were freed up for new customers. It should be noted that while the test has been interpreted widely, punishment of the party in breach is not in itself a legitimate interest.

16.4.2 Sum is not extravagant or unconscionable

The second part of the test will also be a question of fact in each case. There was historically an idea within the law that the amount charged under a liquidated damages clause had to represent a genuine pre-estimate of the loss suffered, but it is clear that this principle no longer holds. The amount due under the clause does not have to be proportional to the actual or potential loss suffered – it has to be proportional to the legitimate interest being protected. Therefore once the court has established the legitimate interest being protected, it must ask whether the amount provided under the clause is extravagant or unconscionable in proportion to that interest. Case law has suggested a number of relevant factors to be considered in deciding this, including:

- The difficulty of proving loss and thus claiming unliquidated damages;
- The difficulty of detecting or litigating individual breaches;
- That breach might also cause loss to third parties;
- That breach might cause a risk of insolvency on the part of the other party;
- That breach might allow the party in breach to make a greater profit;
- That the provision is intended to protect the operation of a legitimate scheme.

16.5 Guarantees and indemnities

Liquidated damages clauses cover the situation where the parties wish to agree in advance the consequences for one party breaching a term of the agreement. Guarantees and indemnities are similar, in that they seek to protect a party against possible future loss, but these provisions relate to protecting a party from loss occasioned by a third party.

A guarantee is a promise by one party, A, to another, B, to be responsible if a third party, C, breaches a contractual obligation to B. If C does breach their obligation, then A has an obligation in turn to make good the loss to B. However, because a guarantee is a secondary obligation dependent on the agreement between B and C, if that contract is set aside for some reason, then A will not be obligated to make good any losses. Contracts of guarantee must be evidenced in writing.[13]

13 S4 Statute of Frauds 1677.

An indemnity is a promise by one party, A, to another, B, to pay the debt of a third party, C. The difference is that an indemnity is a primary obligation, so even if the agreement between B and C is not enforceable, A still remains directly liable for the debt. Contracts of indemnity do not need to be evidenced in writing.

Guarantees and indemnities are usually encountered in situations where one party is acting as a surety for another who is seeking credit (for example, they are taking out a loan). A surety is someone who promises to repay the amount owed if the principal debtor fails to do so as agreed.

Chapter 16 Revision Points

Damages

- Damages are the primary remedy in claims for breach of contract.
- The usual measure of damages is expectation loss – putting the party in the position they should have been in if the contract was performed properly.
- Expectation loss can be calculated in a variety of ways:
  - Difference in value
  - Cost of cure
  - Loss of amenity
  - Loss of a chance
- Also possible to claim for reliance loss – where expectation loss cannot be calculated
- Unliquidated damages = where parties have not agreed damages payable in advance of breach
- Liquidated damages = where parties have agreed amount payable in event of breach
- Court will not uphold penalty clause. Party relying on clause must show:
  - Legitimate interest
  - Sum not extravagant or unconscionable – must be proportionate to the legitimate interest
- Promising to pay for third party
  - Guarantee – secondary obligation
  - Indemnity – primary obligation

It is important to check your knowledge using the following Multiple Choice Questions.

Multiple Choice Questions

Question 1

A ghostwriter who writes autobiographies on behalf of famous people agrees with a celebrity that she will write his autobiography in exchange for a 25% share in all sales of the book. She spends six months conducting research and travelling to interview family and friends of the celebrity. The celebrity then changes his mind and tells the ghostwriter he no longer wishes to proceed with the project.

What measure of damages would be appropriate in this case?

A. Expectation loss based on the difference in value
B. Expectation loss based on the cost of cure
C. Expectation loss based on loss of a chance
D. Reliance loss
E. Liquidated damages

Question 2

A former professional cyclist is retiring from the sport. She intends to sell her racing bike, which was custom made and is worth £15,000. She agrees a contract with her agent, who plans to sell the bike to another one of his clients. The agent agrees to purchase the bike for £14,000.

The agent suffers financial difficulties and is unable to pay the £14,000 as agreed. The professional cyclist is able to sell the bike to a cycling museum for £13,500 instead.

What is the correct measure of damages in this case?

A. No damages can be claimed
B. £500
C. £1,000
D. £1,500
E. £14,000

Question 3

A construction company contract with a professional football club to build the club a new stadium for a total cost of £50 million. It is crucial for the club that the stadium is completed in time for the new season. If it is not, the club will be required to pay another club £500,000 for the right to play at their stadium. In the contract with the construction company, the parties agree a clause which states that if the stadium is not completed on time, the construction company must pay the club £1 million. The stadium is delayed six months in construction and so is not completed on time.

Will the construction company be required to pay the £1 million?

A. Yes, because this is the expectation loss of the club, so £1 million in unliquidated damages is due.
B. Yes, because this is a valid liquidated damages clause. The club has a legitimate interest to protect and the sum is not extravagant or unconscionable.
C. Yes, because a liquidated damages clause will always be upheld in the absence of duress or undue influence.
D. No, because this a penalty clause which cannot be upheld in any circumstances.
E. No, because this is not a valid liquidated damages clause. The club has no legitimate interest to protect and the sum is extravagant.

17 Causation, remoteness, and the duty to mitigate

17.1 Chapter overview

Chapter 16 covered the different bases on which damages can be awarded. However, the law of contract also imposes limitations on what damages can be claimed. This chapter considers those limitations. It begins by considering causation, the requirement that the injured party's loss must be caused by the breach of contract. It then discusses the complex area of remoteness, the principle that losses may only be claimed if they are not too remote from the breach of contract. Finally, the chapter considers the principle of mitigation, which states that the innocent party must take reasonable steps to mitigate (minimise) his or her losses.

17.2 Causation

In order to claim for loss for breach of contract, it must be able to be said that the breach of contract was *a* cause (although not necessarily the sole cause) of the loss. There is no specific test for causation in contract law, with the courts preferring a "common sense" approach.[1] It is possible to "break the chain" of causation in two instances, where something happens between the initial breach and the ultimate loss being suffered. This is where there is:

- An unexpected and unforeseeable act of a third party or other event, which may well have the result of frustrating the contract;
- A voluntary act of the claimant after the breach of contract which caused the particular loss.

Causation is usually straightforward in most cases, with remoteness a more common reason as to why damages cannot be recovered.

1 *Galoo v Bright Grahame Murray* [1994] 1 WLR 1360.

DOI: 10.4324/9781032642161-23

17.3 Remoteness

Consider the following scenario:

> Bartosz, an accountant who runs his own accounting firm, has a contract with Clive under which Clive agrees to service the IT equipment used by Bartosz's company. In breach of the agreement, Clive fails to install appropriate anti-virus software on the computers in Bartosz's offices. One of Bartosz's employees opens an email infected with a virus. The virus locks all of the computers in the office. As a result, Bartosz is unable to carry out a number of regular tasks for clients, losing out on £5,000 in income. Bartosz also has to turn down a special opportunity to complete a tax return for a wealthy celebrity, losing a potential £10,000 in income. Bartosz is also unable to use his office PC to buy some shares he was considering investing in. The shares are now worth double what Bartosz could have bought them for.

Clearly, as a simple matter of causation all of Bartosz's losses were caused by the breach – the computers were locked, so Bartosz could not do the work or buy the shares, so Bartosz lost potential profits. However, as in most areas of law, the law places a limit on what losses can be claimed – a claim cannot be made for losses which are considered "too remote" from the breach. While a claimant can recover damages to place them in the position they expected to be in had the contract been performed properly, remoteness imposes a practical limit on what losses can be claimed.[2]

What exactly is too remote from the breach is a complex question which has led to considerable confusion in the law.

17.3.1 The test for remoteness

What is clear is that the starting point remains the test laid down in the 19th century.[3] The test looks to whether the type of loss being claimed was in the "reasonable contemplation" of *both* parties at the time the contract was made, as a serious possibility in the event of a breach.[4] While this constitutes a single test, it is usually interpreted as being made up of two "limbs".

Losses will not be considered to be too remote if they:

1. Arise naturally, in the usual course of things (usual losses); or
2. Were the result of special circumstances which were known to both parties at the time the contract was made (unusual losses).

2 For expectation loss, see Chapter 16.

3 *Hadley v Baxendale* (1854) 9 Ex 341.

4 *Attorney General of the Virgin Islands v Global Water Associates Ltd (British Virgin Islands)* [2020] UKPC 18.

The practical result of this distinction is that losses under the first "limb" do not need to be specifically pleaded: knowledge of such losses is imputed to the defendant. However, any "special" or "unusual" losses that are out of the ordinary need to specially pleaded and the claimant must show the defendant was aware of these special circumstances at the time the contract was made.

Applying the above to Bartosz, the £5,000 of regular business would certainly fall under the first limb and so would not be considered too remote. Bartosz could claim damages for this loss. The purchase of the shares is not something in the usual course of things, so would not fall under the first limb; and assuming Clive has no knowledge of Bartosz's investment plans, would also not fall under the second limb. The loss is therefore too remote to be claimed. What may be more difficult to classify is the £10,000 lost from the celebrity client. Bartosz will need to show that was a loss within the reasonable contemplation of Clive. He will need to do this either by showing that it was a "normal" enough loss that Clive should have expected it in the usual course of things (the first limb) or, if not, that Clive knew about the celebrity client at the time the contract was made.

17.3.2 Assumption of responsibility

While the two-limbed approach outlined above is usually sufficient to determine whether a loss is too remote, some confusion has been caused by the suggestion of the House of Lords that even where loss is not unusual (and so would be covered by the first limb of the test), it cannot be claimed if the defendant did not assume responsibility for this type of loss.[5]

Case law since this decision has suggested that the "assumption of responsibility" principle will only apply in a small minority of exceptional cases. This may be, for example, where there was clear evidence of a general understanding in a particular trade that a party would not normally be responsible for a particular type of loss.

17.4 Mitigation

Even where the claimant can show losses were caused by the breach and were not too remote from that breach, one further principle may limit the actual amount recovered. This is the principle of mitigation, which is not unique to contract law. This principle is sometimes described as a "duty" to take reasonable steps to mitigate (i.e. minimise or avoid) loss as the result of the defendant's wrongdoing, although it actually covers four distinct situations, as shown in Figure 17.1.

5 *Transfield Shipping Inc v Mercator Shipping Inc (The Achilleas)* [2008] UKHL 48. The matter is made more complicated by the fact that Lords Hoffman and Hope took one approach, Lord Rodger and Baroness Hale took a completely different approach, while Lord Walker purported to be in agreement with both approaches.

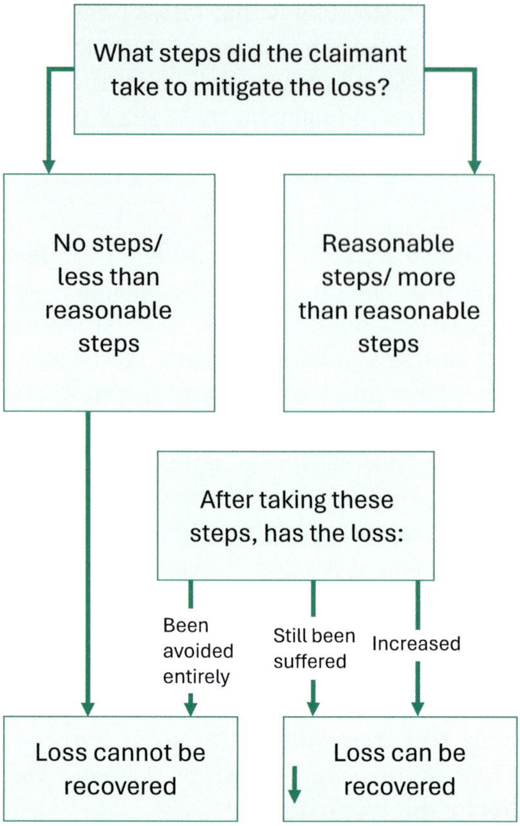

Figure 17.1 Situations involving mitigation of loss

Therefore, mitigation of loss means that where the claimant either was able to avoid loss by taking reasonable steps, or would have avoided loss had reasonable steps been taken, that loss cannot be claimed as damages. Conversely, where the claimant takes reasonable steps and still suffers a loss, the loss may be claimed. Where taking reasonable steps in itself causes the claimant to suffer a greater loss, this additional amount can also be claimed.

The burden of proof in issues of mitigation falls upon the defendant. Thus the defendant must show that the claimant should, as a reasonable person, have taken steps to limit or avoid the loss, and that these steps would have had that effect.

What constitutes reasonable steps is a matter of fact in each case, but it is clear from extensive case law that the standard is relatively low. It is the defendant who has done wrong in committing a breach of contract. A claimant should not be expected to do more than what is reasonable in the ordinary course of business to limit those losses. What is reasonable is judged at the time of the breach, not with the benefit of hindsight.[6] For example, where goods are not delivered, it would be reasonable to seek to purchase the goods elsewhere – but the claimant would not be expected to keep repeatedly checking the market to try and find the absolute best price possible.[7]

Chapter 17 Revision Points

Causation

- Breach must cause loss
- Common sense approach
- Break in chain of causation
  - Act of third party/event
  - Voluntary act of claimant

Remoteness

- Was type of loss in reasonable contemplation?
- First limb: usual course of things
- Second limb: special circumstances
- Assumption of responsibility

Mitigation

- "Duty" to mitigate
- Must take reasonable steps
- Cannot claim if able to mitigate
- Can claim if not able to mitigate/mitigating causes more loss

It is important to check your knowledge using the following Multiple Choice Question.

6 *Banco de Portugal v Waterlow* [1932] AC 452.
7 *Zodiac Maritime Agencies Ltd v Fortescue Metals Group Ltd* [2010] EWHC 903 (Comm).

Multiple Choice Question

Question 1

A company which hires specialist construction equipment contracts with a building firm. Under the contract, the building firm will hire a crane for use on a building project. The building firm tells the hire company that it is crucial the crane is made available for a specific four-week period, as this is when it is required. The building firm also tells the hire company that there is a clause in the contract between the building firm and their client which imposes a penalty of £250,000 on the building firm if the construction is not completed on time.

The crane is supplied two weeks late, and this leads to delays in the building project.

Can the building firm recover the £250,000 penalty from the hire firm?

A. No, because the hire firm did not assume responsibility for the loss.
B. No, because the loss was not in the reasonable contemplation of the hire firm as a loss arising naturally in the usual course of things.
C. No, because the loss was the result of special circumstances which were known to both parties at the time the contract was made.
D. Yes, because the loss was in the reasonable contemplation of the hire firm as a loss arising naturally in the usual course of things.
E. Yes, because the loss was the result of special circumstances which were known to both parties at the time the contract was made.

18 Specific performance and injunctions

18.1 Chapter overview

Chapters 16 and 17 have explained the law relating to the primary remedy for breach of contract, the award of a sum of money in the form of damages. Damages are the common law remedy for breach of contract, but a claimant may also request various remedies from the law of equity. Because these remedies are equitable, they will only be awarded at the discretion of the court. The law has created a number of principles which determine whether these remedies will be available. This chapter will discuss the equitable remedies of specific performance and injunctions. For each remedy, there will be an explanation of what the remedy consists of, its effect on the parties, when it may be awarded, and any bars against the remedy.

18.2 Specific performance

As the name of the remedy suggests, specific performance is a legal order made by a court which requires a party to actually perform a specific contractual obligation.

18.2.1 Effect on the parties

Specific performance has the effect of requiring a party to carry out something which they promised to do under the initial agreement, but which they have failed to do as agreed. This also means that the remedy is limited, in that it can only apply to obligations under the contract – the court cannot order specific performance of anything beyond the obligation(s) in the contract that the party has failed to perform.

In some ways, specific performance may seem to have little adverse effect on a defendant. The defendant is only being compelled to do what he or she initially agreed to, presumably in exchange for valuable consideration. However, the law actually regards specific performance as quite an onerous remedy that will only be awarded in relatively exceptional circumstances. This is a remedy being awarded for a civil wrong (breach of contract) but which forces a defendant to do something, potentially against their will and even against their human rights. A failure to comply with an order for specific performance can even lead to committal to

DOI: 10.4324/9781032642161-24

prison for contempt of court. This has led to very strict controls being placed on when specific performance may be awarded.

18.2.2 Bars against specific performance

Even where the claimant can meet the initial hurdle of demonstrating that damages would not be an adequate remedy, the court may still exercise its discretion to not grant the order of specific performance. Over time, a number of principles have arisen which suggest particular cases and situations where the court will be highly reluctant to grant specific performance as a remedy.

The courts do not grant specific performance in *contracts of personal service*. Where the effect of an order would be to force the defendant to personally perform a service, the remedy is unavailable because it would unfairly infringe on that person's liberty.[1] In particular, this means that an employee will not be forced to work for an employer against their will.[2] It also means that specific performance will not usually be ordered where a contract relies on a personal relationship of mutual confidence which has broken down.

The court will also be reluctant to award specific performance where to do so would require *constant supervision*. This usually applies where the order covers continuous duties (as opposed to a one-off duty, such as transferring goods), and so there is a danger that parties will repeatedly return to court to argue about whether the contract is being performed. Similarly, the court will not award specific performance if what constitutes performance is imprecise or unclear.[3]

Because specific performance is an equitable remedy, the usual *equitable maxims* apply. This means that, for example, the party seeking the order must come to equity with "clean hands" – any wrongdoing on their own part means they are unlikely to gain an equitable remedy such as specific performance. The need to do equity also means that the remedy will not be granted where to do so would cause severe hardship to the defendant, or there is no "mutuality" in the agreement – meaning where the defendant being ordered to perform could not claim in turn if the claimant breached the contract.

18.2.3 When specific performance may be awarded

In order for specific performance to be available as a potential remedy, the claimant must demonstrate why the court should depart from the usual remedy of damages. As such, to successfully claim the remedy, the claimant has to first show that damages would be in some way inadequate.

1 *De Francesco v Barnum* (1890) 45 Ch D 430.
2 Initially a common law rule, this is now confirmed by S236 Trade Union and Labour Relations (Consolidation) Act 1992.
3 See for example *Co-operative Insurance Society Ltd v Argyll Stores (Holdings) Ltd* [1998] AC 1 where the House of Lords refused to grant an order requiring the defendant to keep a store open in a shopping centre for the next 25 years.

It may be that *payment of damages would be of little or no use* to the claimant. This can occur in a number of situations.

- If the contract is one for the sale of land, specific performance will be available. This is because no two pieces of land are identical – for example, if someone makes an agreement to buy the house of their dreams, the seller cannot simply offer money to purchase a different house. Contracts for the sale of land are considered unique, so specific performance would still be available even in a situation where an almost identical piece of land could be offered (for example, the seller is a property developer who also built an identical house next door).
- In other contracts to supply goods, specific performance may be available if the claimant can show the goods are sufficiently unique.[4]
- Specific performance may also be available if the claimant cannot easily purchase the goods or services elsewhere in the market, even if they are not truly unique. This may be because the goods themselves are unusual (for example, a contract for the purchase of a ship) or because they could not be obtained within a reasonable time.[5]

It might instead be that the court itself *cannot properly quantify the level of damages*. As you learned in Chapter 16, there are various measures by which damages can be calculated but there remain cases where it is not possible to put a meaningful figure on the loss suffered.

Finally, it may be that *substantive damages cannot be recovered* by the claimant. This might be because:

- Damages awarded would only be nominal, because while there had been a significant breach it had not caused direct financial loss to the claimant[6];
- Damages were excluded or significantly limited as a potential remedy by a term of the contract[7];
- Damages would not in practice be recoverable, for example because enforcement would need to take place in a foreign country or because the defendant would not be able to actually pay the sum required.[8]

18.3 Injunctions

Like specific performance, an injunction is an order made by the court, and it is an equitable remedy, so only granted at the court's discretion. The difference is that an injunction does not need to relate to an existing term of the contract. Indeed,

4 See *Gregor Fisken Ltd v Carl* [2020] EWHC 1385 (Comm) for a modern example (order granted for specific performance of delivery up of a gearbox for a rare Ferrari car).
5 See for example *Sky Petroleum Ltd v VIP Petroleum Ltd* [1974] 1 WLR 576.
6 See for example *Beswick v Beswick* [1968] AC 58, discussed in more detail in Chapter 4.
7 See for example *AB v CD* [2014] EWCA Civ 229.
8 See for example *The Laemthong Glory* [2004] EWHC 2738 (Comm).

an injunction is simply an order that a party either must do something (a mandatory injunction) or must not do something (a prohibitory injunction).

18.3.1 Effect on the parties

As stated above, the effect of an injunction on the party named is to either compel them to do something or prohibit them from doing something. Failing to comply with an injunction may be a contempt of court.

When the court awards an injunction, it is important to distinguish between interim injunctions and final injunctions. An interim injunction is one granted before trial and will only take effect until trial, at the conclusion of which the court will either lift the injunction or award a final injunction. Interim injunctions will usually only be awarded where there is a risk of harm between the application and the trial that could not be ultimately compensated by damages.

18.3.2 When an injunction may be awarded

Because mandatory injunctions in contract law would usually relate to ordering the defendant to do something they had agreed to do under the contract, they are in such cases treated very similarly to specific performance and the same rules outlined above would apply.

The other situation where a mandatory injunction might be requested is after breach has occurred and where the claimant wants the court to order the defendant to do something to make up for the breach. In such cases the court applies a "balance of convenience" test: does the prejudice suffered by the defendant in granting the injunction outweigh the benefit gained by the claimant?[9]

The particular value of prohibitory injunctions in contract law is to prevent a future breach of contract. As such, prohibitory injunctions can only be used to enforce a negative obligation – a contractual promise not to do something. Such injunctions may be granted where to do so would not be "oppressive" to the defendant.

18.3.3 Bars against injunctive relief

Much the same bars outlined above in relation to specific performance will apply to injunctions.

9 *Sharp v Harrison* [1922] 1 Ch 502.

Chapter 18 Revision Points

Specific performance

- Equitable remedy
  - At discretion of court
- Damages must be inadequate
  - Sale of land
  - Unique goods
  - Very hard to obtain substitute
  - Cannot quantify damages
  - Nominal damages only
  - Defendant cannot pay
  - Cannot enforce against defendant
- Bars
  - Contract for personal service
  - Constant supervision
  - Equitable bars

Injunctions

- Equitable remedy
  - At discretion of court
- Two types
  - Mandatory
  - Prohibitory
- Mandatory – must do something
  - Rare/hard to obtain
  - Balance of convenience test
- Prohibitory – must not do something
  - Prevent future breach
  - Oppressive to defendant test

It is important to check your knowledge using the following Multiple Choice Question.

Multiple Choice Question

Question 1

A politician commissions a famous artist to paint a portrait of her giving a speech at a party conference. After agreeing to paint the picture, the artist is then upset by one of the politician's policies and decides to not paint the picture.

Can the politician obtain an order of specific performance against the artist?

A. Yes, because damages would not be a sufficient remedy.
B. Yes, because the contract requires constant supervision.
C. No, because damages would be a sufficient remedy.
D. No, because specific performance is not granted in contracts for personal services.
E. No, because the politician does not have "clean hands" due to the unpopular policy.

19 Basic principles of restitution and unjust enrichment in the context of termination of contract

19.1 Chapter overview

This chapter will discuss restitution and unjust enrichment in terms of repudiatory breach and its relevance to unjust enrichment and the purpose of damages. It will also discuss how the courts award damages on a *quantum meruit* basis.

19.2 Restitutionary damages

As discussed in Chapter 16, the purpose of contractual damages is usually to put the claimant back in the position they would have been in had the contract not been breached. This is done by calculating the expectation loss. However, restitutionary damages cover unjust enrichment at the expense of the other party because of a deliberate breach of contract which has resulted in the wrongdoer gaining profits from the actual breach. In other words, rather than compensating the claimant for a loss they have suffered, they instead allow the claimant to claim for a gain that the defendant has received.

Restitutionary damages are therefore an exceptional remedy that is only available where there is evidence of unjust enrichment, or the defendant has directly benefited from committing the legal wrong of breach of contract. Without that, contractual damages will not compensate a party where that party has not suffered any loss.

Consider the following two scenarios:

> *Pamela agrees to sell Brenda a computer for use in Brenda's business. In breach of contract, Pamela supplies a defective computer that constantly crashes while being used. Brenda loses out on £5,000 of business because of the problems with the defective computer. Brenda knows that Pamela's computer sales business is very successful and believes that she should be entitled to more than £5,000, because Pamela made profits of £25 million last year.*

In this scenario, Pamela's profits are irrelevant. The breach of contract has led to a specific loss – £5,000 – and this is the amount that Brenda can claim from Pamela.

DOI: 10.4324/9781032642161-25

> *Arnold enters a contract with Gerald to build a block of flats on Gerald's land. Gerald stipulates in the form of a covenant that he only wants Arnold to build 50 flats. In deliberate breach of the restrictive covenant, Arnold builds 60 flats as he knows this would be more profitable. Arnold sues and wants an injunction which is subsequently refused as the work has been completed. Arnold makes a profit from the additional 10 flats but there is no loss to Gerald. Can Arnold claim for damages?*

In this situation, there is a clear relationship between the wrong committed by Arnold (breaching the contract with Gerald) and a substantial extra profit Arnold has made. It could be considered unjust that Arnold has made this profit by doing something he explicitly promised not to do, and so the law of restitution may assist.

19.3 Account of profits

Under this head of damages, the potentially recoverable losses are those losses from which the defendant or claimant would have benefitted. In a claim under this head, the breaching party is required to account for the profits they have made as a result of breaching the original contract. The focus here is looking at the gains and benefits the defendant has made in breach of contract. It is argued that these principles go against traditional remedies for breach of contract because they punish the party in breach rather than placing the non-breaching in the position they would have been had the breach not occurred. As a result, such damages are only awarded in exceptional circumstances. It is not sufficient in itself that the breach of contract was cynical and deliberate or that it allowed the defendant to make a profit elsewhere – it must be shown that *the claimant's objective interest in performance of the relevant obligation makes it just and equitable that the defendant should retain no benefit from the breach of the obligation*. Otherwise the remedy awarded would be disproportionate to the wrong done to the claimant, because the claimant is being given damages above and beyond their own financial loss.

Consider the following scenario:

> Jane is a senior intelligence officer who works for a government agency investigating domestic terrorism. As part of her contract of employment, Jane is strictly prohibited from revealing any information about ongoing investigations. Jane decides to write a book about her life, in which she openly discusses various ongoing investigations and reveals secret information such as the names of confidential informants providing information to the agency. Jane's book is a huge success and she makes large profits from its sale.[1]

1 See *Attorney-General v Blake* [2001] 1 AC 268 on which the facts of this scenario are based.

A situation like Jane's is one where an account for profits may be awarded. The government agency have a crucial interest in Jane not revealing secrets relating to national security. The court may consider that in these circumstances, it would just and equitable that Jane receives no benefit from breaching such an important obligation. It is clear from case law that a commercial interest is very unlikely to meet this strict test; it is more likely in cases like Jane's where the claimant's interest is more sensitive that being purely financial.[2] An account of profits for breach of contract will also only usually be awarded where there is a fiduciary relationship (or a similar relationship of trust and confidence) between the parties.[3]

19.4 Negotiating damages

This head of damages is sometimes called "*Wrotham Park* damages" after the case where such losses were first awarded.[4] It is similar to an account of profits in that it seeks to make the defendant pay the claimant a sum relating to the defendant's breach of contract; but it is distinct in that unlike account of profits, negotiating damages do directly compensate for loss.

Negotiating damages are awarded to compensate for the loss of a valuable contractual right. They are awarded when Party A contracts with B and Party B promises to do or not do something. Party B then breaches that obligation and makes a profit. In order to place a financial value on the contractual "right" that has been lost, the court awards damages by hypothetically negotiating reasonably between the parties. Hypothetically, what would it have cost for the breaching party to instead have agreed with the innocent party that that party would waive their contractual right?

Consider this example of Arnold and Gerald given above. Gerald does not have any less money in his bank account now Arnold has built 60 flats than he would had Arnold built 50 flats. It seems his expectation loss is zero. However, Arnold has built an extra 10 flats, in breach of Gerald's contractual right to limit the building to 50 flats. So Gerald has suffered a loss – his right to limit the number of flats built. The court could consider how much it would have cost Gerald to negotiate with Arnold to amend the contract to allow Gerald to build the extra 10 flats.

19.5 Payment on a *quantum meruit* basis

As discussed in Chapter 15 performance must be precise and exact, in other words complete performance. Where performance falls short of substantial performance, there will be some benefit to one party potentially without payment for the

2 *Experience Hendrix LLC v PPX Enterprises Inc* [2003] EWCA Civ 323.
3 *Morris-Garner v One Step (Support) Ltd* [2018] UKSC 20.
4 *Wrotham Park Estate Co v Parkside Homes Ltd* [1974] 2 All ER 321.

benefit received from the performing party. The claimant in these circumstances would receive the benefit and would be unjustly enriched by the performing party. This term is referred to as *quantum meruit* ("as much as it deserves") and means that a reasonable sum is to be awarded to the performing party for the work carried out to account for the benefit conferred to the claimant. This is also the case with partial performance and wrongful prevention of performance (discussed further in Chapter 15). This principle is based on restitution compared to normal damages for breach of contract as its purpose is not to compensate for losses arising from the breach but rather pay (a reasonable sum) the performing party for the work performed.[5]

Consider this example:

> Sean is a famous singer who contracts with Alexis to perform a series of 15 concerts at an arena owned by Alexis. The contract is expressed to be an entire contract – Sean will only be paid once he completes all 15 contracts. After 9 concerts, Sean suddenly retires from music and refuses to perform the remaining 6 concerts.

Clearly, Sean has not completely performed the contract. It seems unlikely that Sean has substantially performed the contract either – Alexis cannot "make good" the other six concerts. The contract is not frustrated, because Sean has chosen not to continue with it – it is his "fault". As such, it seems clear that the contract has been breached, not performed.

Yet Alexis has had the benefit of nine contracts and presumably has made large profits from these concerts. It would also seem unjust if Alexis had to pay Sean nothing at all. In this instance, a *quantum meruit* payment seems appropriate.

Chapter 19 Revision Points

- Restitution damages
- Account of profits
- Negotiating damages
- Payment on a *quantum meruit* basis

It is important to check your knowledge using the following Multiple Choice Question.

5 *See Cutter v Powell* [1795] 6 Term Reports 320 which this scenario is loosely based on.

Multiple Choice Question

Question 1

Eze has contracted with David on 2 January to install a new kitchen in his house for £10,000. The price is to be paid on completion. Eze has bought all the materials. Eze and David agree on the contract price and set a date for completion. David is due to start the work the following week but before he starts, he informs Eze he can no longer carry out his contractual obligations, as he has been offered a lucrative contract with a property developer to renovate kitchens in a new development over the next 12 months for £120,000. David informs Eze that it is not possible for him to take on Eze's kitchen, as his new contract starts next week. Eze finds another carpenter, but he charges £15,000.

Which of the following best describes the legal position?

A. Eze has a strong claim against David for an account of profits but not the £5,000.
B. Eze has a strong claim against David for £5,000, and for an account of profits.
C. Eze has no claim against David, because David has withdrawn from the contract prior to commencing performance.
D. Eze has a strong claim against David for £5,000, but will not have a claim for an account of profits.
E. Eze should seek the remedy of specific performance to force David to install the kitchen.

20 Key cases in contract law

20.1 Formation of contract

20.1.1 Offer and acceptance

Carlill v Carbolic Smoke Ball Co *[1892] 1 QB 256*

The facts were:

The Carbolic Smoke Ball Company advertised medication that allegedly prevented people contracting influenza (flu) during an epidemic. The advert stated that anyone that took the ball as prescribed and caught influenza would be rewarded with a payment of £100. To prove their sincerity, the company deposited £1,000 with the Alliance Bank. The claimant, Mrs Carlill, bought the smoke ball, used it as prescribed, and caught influenza. Mrs Carlill claimed the £100. The company refused to honour the payment stating that the advert was not an offer, and the advert was not intended to be taken seriously but rather a "sales puff" which had no legal consequences.

The dispute to be decided by the court was:

The defendants argued that there was no contract as the essential elements of a contract were not satisfied, and therefore the £100 reward promise by the Carbolic Smoke Ball Company should not be paid to Mrs Carlill. They argued that the advert was merely an invitation to treat, and that in any event it was impossible to "contract with the whole world" as it was not addressed to a specific person.

Use these questions to analyse the legal issues:

- Why was the deposit of £1,000 significant in the ruling?
- Why is this an exception to the general rule in relation to an advertisement?
- Was this a unilateral and/or bilateral contract? What is the difference between the two?

The principle of law applied/established was:

Advertisements are usually invitations to treat. This is because most advertisements do not contain clear and certain terms, are not made with the intention

DOI: 10.4324/9781032642161-26

to be bound on acceptance, and often are selling goods of which there is limited stock. However, this presumption can be overturned in a particular case depending on the circumstances. Some advertisements can constitute a unilateral offer rather than an invitation to treat and such an offer can be made to the world.

The outcome (the principle that applied to the facts) was:

It was decided that there was a valid contract. The offer terms were clear and specific enough to constitute an offer. The offer was addressed to consumers that bought the smoke ball and took it as and when prescribed, and who then caught flu anyway, so there was only a limited number of people who could accept it (by performance). The intention to form a legally binding contract was evidenced by the deposit of the £1,000 put in the Alliance Bank.

Notes:

This case was of particular importance in consumer advertising practice and transactions prior to the introduction of consumer legislation to protect consumers from unfair practices.

Gibson v Manchester City Council *[1979] 1 WLR 294*

The facts were:

The claimant, a council tenant, wanted to purchase his council house during a time where there was a "Right to Buy" scheme available. There was a series of correspondence by letter. In one of the letters, it stated that "the Corporation may be prepared to sell to sell the house to [Mr Gibson] at £2,180 . . .". The letter instructed Mr Gibson that if he was interested in purchasing his council house, he was to complete the necessary paperwork and return it to the council. Mr Gibson completed the relevant paperwork and returned it. By then there was a change of policy, and because of this, the council refused to sell Mr Gibson the house.

The dispute to be decided by the court was:

The court had to decide whether the language used during the negotiations to sell the council house to Mr Gibson was definite enough to constitute an offer to Mr Gibson to buy the council house (if so, returning the paperwork would constitute acceptance).

Use these questions to analyse the legal issues:

- What was important about the language used during the negotiation process?
- Why were the words "may be prepared to sell" so important?

The principle of law applied/established was:

The use of language is crucial during the negotiation stages when contracting. In order to constitute an offer, clear evidence showing an intention to be bound upon acceptance by the other party must be present.

The outcome (the principle that applied to the facts) was:

There was no binding contract as the council's letter did not show sufficient intention to constitute an offer. The words "may be prepared to sell" were crucial in determining that the initial correspondence amounted to an invitation to treat. The council's letter was regarded as an invitation to treat, inviting an offer from Mr Gibson, rather than a valid offer.

Notes:

In a case on similar facts, *Storer v Manchester City Council* [1974] 1 WLR 1403, the language used by the Council was clear and certain in a document headed "Agreement for Sale" which amounted to a valid offer which Mr Storer accepted, and therefore constituted a binding contract between Mr Storer and Manchester City Council.

20.1.2 Intention to create legal relations, certainty, and capacity

Balfour v Balfour *[1918] 2 KB 571*

The facts were:

A husband had to go abroad to work in Sri Lanka. His wife was advised to stay in England because of her health. As his wife could not travel, he verbally promised to pay her £30 per month for maintenance until she joined him in Sri Lanka. The husband stopped making payments and the couple eventually decided to separate. The wife issued legal proceedings arguing that Mr Balfour was bound by the promise to pay £30 per month.

The dispute to be decided by the court was:

The court had to decide whether the agreement to pay £30 per month maintenance was legally enforceable between the husband and wife.

Use these questions to analyse the legal issues:

- What is the rebuttable presumption in social or domestic agreements?
- What was the relationship between husband and wife at the time of the agreement?

The principle of law applied/established was:

In a social or domestic agreement, the rebuttable presumption is that there is no intention to create legal relations.

The outcome (the principle that applied to the facts) was:

The agreement was not enforceable, and the wife could not recover the money because the agreement lacked intent. It was an oral, informal agreement made between a married couple who at the time were not separated. Therefore, there was no legally binding agreement.

Notes:

It is possible to rebut the presumption in a social or domestic context. This is demonstrated in *Merritt v Merritt* [1970] 1 WLR 1211 where the agreement was in writing and part of a divorce settlement.

20.1.3 Consideration and variation of contract

Chappell & Co. v Nestle *[1960] AC 87*

The facts were:

Nestle ran a promotion where people who purchased chocolate bars could return the used wrappers to Nestle with a small amount of money to enable them to receive a vinyl record of a popular song.

The dispute to be decided by the court was:

The court had to decide whether Nestle were obliged to pay royalties to Chappell (as they owned the copyright in the song) as part of the promotion. The legal question was whether the chocolate wrappers amounted to consideration in the eyes of the law (and thus created a contract). Nestle argued that as the wrappers were thrown away, they were not worth anything and therefore did not amount to consideration.

Use these questions to analyse the legal issues:

- Was this sufficient consideration?
- Was this adequate consideration?

The principle of law applied/established was:

Consideration must be sufficient but not adequate. As Lord Somervell stated in his judgment in the case:

> "A contracting party can stipulate for what consideration he chooses. A peppercorn does not cease to be good consideration if it is established that the

promisee does not like pepper and will throw away the corn". Consideration can be anything stipulated by the promisor.

The outcome (the principle that applied to the facts) was:

The chocolate wrappers amounted to sufficient consideration as they had some (very minimal) economic value in the eyes of law. It was irrelevant that this value was very low, because consideration only needs to be sufficient, not adequate.

Notes:

You might notice that supermarket vouchers and similar schemes sometimes state they have a value of 0.01 pence. This is a legal device to ensure that the terms and conditions of the vouchers are legally enforceable – because by stating these pieces of paper to have a sufficient value, they can be valid consideration.

Foakes v Beer *(1884) 9 App Cas 605*

The facts were:

Dr Foakes borrowed £2,090 from Mrs Beer, on the agreement that Dr Foakes would repay £2,390 (including interest on the loan). It was later agreed between the parties that Foakes would pay by instalments and would only repay the initial loan, not the interest. Mrs Beer then changed her mind and sued for the outstanding interest.

The dispute to be decided by the court was:

Was the second agreement, to repay £2,090 rather than £2,390, supported by consideration?

Use these questions to analyse the legal issues:

- Why is consideration a requirement for a variation in contract?
- What was Mrs Beer promising to do in the second agreement
- What was Dr Foakes promising to do in the second agreement?

The principle of law applied/established was:

A variation of contract must be supported by fresh consideration. Part payment of a debt is not satisfaction for the whole.

The outcome (the principle that applied to the facts) was:

Under the initial agreement, both parties provided consideration. Mrs Beer promised to give Dr Foakes £2,090 now, and Dr Foakes promised in return to pay £2,390 back to her later. However, under the second agreement Mrs Beer provided a benefit to Dr Foakes – letting him avoid giving her the extra £300 in interest – but all Dr Foakes promised to do was pay money to Mrs Beer that he was already contractually obligated to pay her. As such, he did not provide fresh consideration, the second agreement was thus not valid, and he still owed her the £300 .

Notes:

There is still debate about the different rules in terms of payments to pay less and payments to pay more in terms of "practical benefit". The Supreme Court had the opportunity in *Rock Advertising Ltd v MWB Business Exchange Centres Ltd* [2018] UKSC 24 to address this discrepancy, but chose not to do so.

20.1.4 Privity of contract and rights of third parties

Beswick v Beswick *[1968] AC 58*

The facts were:

The owner of a company agreed to sell the company to his nephew (the defendant). In exchange, the nephew promised to pay his uncle a salary as a consultant for the company for the rest of his life. The nephew also promised that on the death of his uncle, he would pay his uncle's widow, the claimant, £5 a week for the rest of her life.

During the uncle's lifetime, the defendant paid the salary agreed. On the uncle's death, the defendant made one payment of £5 and then stopped paying his aunt. Importantly, the claimant Mrs Beswick was named as the executor of her late husband's estate.

The dispute to be decided by the court was:

The claim was brought by Mrs Beswick both in her own name, as the person who was intended to benefit from the contract, and in her capacity as executor of Mr Beswick's estate. Could the contract be enforced by Mrs Beswick in either capacity; and if so, what remedy was available?

Use these questions to analyse the legal issues:

- How does the principle of privity limit the rights of a third party to enforce a contract?
- What financial loss had the uncle, Mr Beswick, suffered?
- What alternative remedy could be awarded instead of damages, in a case of breach of contract?

The principle of law applied/established was:

> The principle of privity of contract is clear in holding that a third party cannot sue (or be sued) on a contract to which they are not a party.

A contract can be enforced by the parties to it. Where appropriate, the court can, at its discretion, grant the equitable remedy of specific performance to the non-breaching party, as an alternative to damages.

The outcome (the principle applied to the facts) was:

> Because of privity, Mrs Beswick had no right to enforce the contract in her own name. It did not matter that the contract was for her benefit – she was not a party to it, so had no contractual rights.

However, as executor of her husband's estate, she "stood in his shoes". He was a party to the contract, so he (and after his death, his estate) could enforce it. There was no reason not to grant specific performance and it would be inequitable not to award the remedy, given the nephew's promise to pay Mrs Beswick was an important part of the consideration provided to buy the business.

Notes:

> *Beswick* was decided on appeal to the House of Lords, but in the Court of Appeal below Lord Denning and Danckwerts LJ had argued that the entire concept of privity could be implied to have been overturned by particular wording in the Law of Property Act 1925. The House of Lords was unanimous in rejecting this argument. However, two of the Law Lords (Lord Reid and Lord Pearce) made strong comments in favour of law reform to allow a third party to enforce a contract made for their benefit. This reform eventually came in the form of the Contracts (Rights of Third Parties) Act 1999.

20.2 Contents of a contract

20.2.1 Express terms and incorporation of terms

Dick Bentley Productions Ltd v Harold Smith (Motors) Ltd *[1965] 1 WLR 623*

The facts were:

> The claimant purchased a second-hand luxury car from the defendant. The defendant told the claimant that he was in a position to know the history of

the car, which had mainly been used in Germany. The defendant told the claimant that the car had been fitted with a replacement engine and gearbox, and that since that point it had travelled 20,000 miles. After the claimant bought the car, he had a number of problems with its performance. It was established at trial that the car had probably driven around 100,000 miles since the engine replacement.

The dispute to be decided by the court was:

Was the statement about the mileage of the car a term or a representation?

Use these questions to analyse the legal issues:

- What tests can the court use to determine whether a pre-contractual statement could be incorporated as a term of the contract?
- On these facts, was there anything in particular about the defendant's behaviour that suggested the statement was a term?

The principle of law applied/established was:

When the party making a pre-contractual statement is in a better position to determine the truth of that statement, it is more likely to be incorporated as a term in the contract.

The outcome (the principle applied to the facts) was:

The statement as to the mileage of the car was a term. The defendant had told the claimant he was in a position to know the history of the car. He could, had he chosen to do so, have found out the true position. The claimant relied on this special knowledge of the defendant in making his decision to enter into the contract.

Notes:

In his judgment, Lord Denning contrasted the earlier case of *Oscar Chess Ltd v Williams* [1957] 1 WLR 370 which also involved statements made during the sale of a second-hand car. In the *Oscar Chess* case, the seller had been given a log-book when he originally bought the car which stated that the car was manufactured in 1948. The seller, who had no special knowledge of cars, believed the log-book and when he in turn sold the car, he told the buyer that the car was a 1948 model. It transpired the car was actually an older model. Lord Denning noted that in *Oscar Chess* the court found the statement was only a misrepresentation, because the person making it had no special knowledge and was in no better position to find out the truth of his statement than the buyer.

Thornton v Shoe Lane Parking *[1971] 2 QB 163*

The facts were:

The claimant parked his car at a car park operated by the defendant. Outside the car park was a notice setting out the charges for parking and excluding liability for theft. The claimant drove up to the entrance and took a ticket from the automated machine. He then drove into the car park and parked. On returning to his car later that day, there was an accident and he suffered extensive personal injuries. On the ticket given to the claimant by the automated machine, there was small print stating the ticket was issued subject to conditions available on the premises. These conditions were on a notice inside the car park, and included a clause excluding liability for personal injury.

The dispute to be decided by the court was:

- Could the car park operator rely on the exclusion clause included on the conditions posted in the car park?
- Was the exclusion clause incorporated into the contract at the time of contracting?

Use these questions to analyse the legal issues:

- In order to incorporate a term by notice, what are the requirements?
- At what point did the claimant make his contract with the defendant?

The principle of law applied/established was:

In order to incorporate a term by reasonable notice, that notice must be provided before or at the time the contract is made.

The outcome (the principle applied to the facts) was:

The contract was made when the claimant drove up to the car park entrance and took a ticket from the automated machine. The machine itself acted as a standing offer, which the claimant accepted by taking a ticket from the machine and entering the car park. Therefore, the terms posted outside by the machine were incorporated into the contract (the charges, and exclusion of liability for theft). However, the contract was made at that point, so the notice inside the car park, which the claimant could only see after taking a ticket and entering, came too late, in other words after the contract had been formed and not at the time of contracting. Therefore the exclusion clause relating to personal injury was not incorporated and was ineffective.

Even if the clause was not held to be incorporated too late, this was also a case where the degree of notice provided was insufficient. The clause was very wide and restricted the claimant's legal rights, so it needed to be brought to the claimant's attention rather than being contained in very small print in a large block of text.

Notes:

This case was heard in 1970, so it predates the Unfair Contract Terms Act 1977 (and the Consumer Rights Act 2015). Today, these statutes would prevent a clause excluding liability for personal injury caused by the defendant's negligence, even if it had been incorporated into the contract.

20.2.2 Implied terms

Marks & Spencer Plc v BNP Paribas Securities Services Trust Co (Jersey) Ltd *[2015] UKSC 72*

The facts were:

The claimant rented offices in a building in central London from the defendant landlord. The lease included a "break clause" which allowed the tenant to end the lease early on a particular date. The tenant exercised the break clause and the lease ended in January 2012. However, the claimant had paid rent up to March 2012. There was nothing in the contract to indicate the "extra" rent should be repaid.

The dispute to be decided by the court was:

Would a term be implied into the contract to the effect that if the tenant exercised the break clause, the landlord would repay any rent received for the period after the lease came to an end?

Use these questions to analyse the legal issues:

- Would the contract make business sense without the implied term?
- Was the term so obvious it went without saying?

The principle of law applied/established was:

Despite commentary suggesting otherwise, the law had not changed in regards to the tests for implying a term in fact. Implication of a term was a separate process to interpretation of the contract. Interpretation might consider what was reasonable between the parties, but implication of terms looked instead at what was necessary (and so was a stricter test).

To imply a term in fact, the term must meet one of two tests:

1. The business efficacy test – is the term needed to make the contract make business sense?
2. The officious bystander test – is the term so obvious that it goes without saying?

It is irrelevant whether implying a term would make the contract fairer or more commercially sensible or viable. It must meet one of the traditional tests (and in most cases, meeting one will also mean meeting the other).

The outcome (the principle applied to the facts) was:

> The payment of rent is in exchange for the use and enjoyment of the property, so there was a strong argument that it would be unfair or unreasonable for the landlord to be able to retain rent paid for a period during which the claimant would not actually have the use of the property. Because when rent was due was based on a separate agreement, the parties did not negotiate the lease with knowledge as to whether the break clause would take effect just before or just after a rent payment.

On the other hand, the lease was a detailed document entered into between two large and experienced businesses. It had been negotiated and drafted by expert solicitors on both sides. The contract covered many other eventualities, so it could be argued that if the parties had wanted to include a term along the lines of the one the claimant wanted to be implied, they would have done so.

Ultimately, the term was not required to make the contract make business sense. The contract functioned perfectly well without the term, albeit in a way that could be seen as unfair to the claimant. There was no evidence that both parties (particularly the defendant) intended that the rent would be returned in this situation, especially given that there was long-standing legal authority to the effect that a landlord could retain rent paid in advance. Therefore, the term was not implied.

Notes:

> While the Supreme Court was at pains to point out it was not overruling the case, the decision in *Marks & Spencer* was considered by many to be a rebuttal of comments made by the Privy Council in *Attorney General of Belize v Belize Telecom Ltd* [2009] UKPC 10. In the *Belize Telecom* case, Lord Hoffmann suggested implication and interpretation were part of the same process, leading to academics arguing that the test for implying a term in fact had been weakened from what was necessary to what was reasonable. The *Marks & Spencer* decision clearly stated that the traditional approach to implying terms in fact had not altered.

20.2.3 The interpretation of terms

Wood v Capita Insurance Services Ltd *[2017] UKSC 24*

The facts were:

> The defendant had entered into a contract to purchase the claimant's business, which insured classic cars. A term of the purchase agreement warranted

that the company had not broken any applicable financial services laws. This term had a two-year time limit for the buyer to enforce.

A separate term (an "indemnity clause") stated that the sellers would reimburse the buyer for any compensation the company had to pay "arising out of claims or complaints registered with [the regulatory authorities]" about mis-selling of insurance before the sale of the company.

Shortly after the purchase of the company, the defendant was made aware that there had been potential mis-selling of insurance. For some time prior to the purchase, the insurance company had been quoting a lower price on comparison websites, but had then used unfair sales tactics to force customers to agree to a higher price when they actually bought the insurance policy.

The defendant reported what had happened to the regulatory authorities. The company and the regulator agreed a compensation scheme to pay customers who had been affected by the mis-selling. In response to a separate claim by the claimant, the defendant counter-claimed for the money it had had to pay out under the compensation scheme.

The dispute to be decided by the court was:

The defendant did not claim in time to rely on the warranty that was time limited. So the claim was brought solely on the indemnity clause. This stated that the claimant would have to pay when compensation arose from a claim or complaint by a customer. But the compensation scheme actually came about because the company's own management reported the mis-selling. Should the indemnity clause be interpreted to cover the loss?

Use these questions to analyse the legal issues:

- Looking at the actual words used in the indemnity clause, did it cover loss arising out of a claim or complaint?
- Looking at the wider context, did the parties intend for the indemnity clause to cover all losses or only those from claims or complaints?

The principle of law applied/established was:

When interpreting a term, the court's tasks is to ascertain the objective meaning of the language which the parties have chosen to use. This is a "unitary exercise", meaning that the court has to look at a range of factors including the factual background and the quality of the drafting before choosing the interpretation which is most consistent with business common sense.

The outcome (the principle applied to the facts) was:

> The clause was ambiguous in its wording and could have been drafted more clearly. The court should look at both the text of the clause and the wider context as part of the unitary approach. The text of the clause restricted it to situations where there was a claim by a consumer. The wider context was that there was a much wider warranty which would cover other issues (but which had a two-year time limit). It was important to note that the contract had been drafted by expert lawyers.

It made commercial common sense that the parties included a wider clause that covered all liabilities for mis-selling, but that was limited by time; and a separate clause that certain liabilities (i.e. those arising from a consumer claim or complaint) would be indemnified without a time limit. Therefore, the term was interpreted to not cover the loss suffered by the defendant.

Notes:

> The defendant buyers were badly affected by the existence of the time limited warranty. Had they claimed within two years, that warranty would have covered their losses. Had that warranty not existed, it may have been that the court were more willing to widely interpret the indemnity clause.

20.3 Vitiating elements

20.3.1 Misrepresentation

Esso Petroleum Co Ltd v Mardon *[1976] 2 All ER 5*

The facts were:

> Mr Mardon leased a petrol station from Esso. During negotiations for the lease Mr Mardon was assured by Esso's representative that the annual sales would be 20,000 gallons of petrol per year. The forecast was based on a busy road where the customers accessed the site. However, road alterations (which Esso were aware of) had meant that the entrance changed. The petrol station was now accessible through a side street which was not visible; this meant that fewer customers would use the petrol station. The estimate was not revised, and as a result, the sales were not as expected and the petrol station became unviable to run due to the relocation of the pumps. As a result, Mardon could not afford to repay the loan from Esso, which then claimed for the rent and sought repossession of the garage. Mardon then counter-claimed and argued that there had been a negligent misrepresentation made by Esso.

The dispute to be decided by the court was:

The court had to decide whether the statement about the takings made by Esso's representative merely amounted to an unactionable statement of opinion and not an actionable statement of fact.

Use these questions to analyse the legal issues:

- What is the usual rule about statements of opinion?
- What was crucial about the relationship between Esso's expert and an average person?

The principle of law applied/established was:

Where the maker of a statement has specialist expertise and experience, the statements made during pre-contractual negotiations will amount to a statement of fact and not an opinion, as the person making the statement possesses greater skill and knowledge than the other person.

The outcome (the principle that applied to the facts) was:

The statement made by Esso's representative was not a statement of opinion but rather a statement of fact as Esso's representative had substantial experience and possessed greater skill in estimating potential sales. Furthermore, any changes to the estimate should have been notified to Mardon.

Notes:

In cases where the statement maker does not have skill or knowledge, the pre-contractual statement may well amount to an opinion as illustrated in *Bisset v Wilkinson* [1927] AC 177, where a seller of a sheep farm did not have substantial skill or experience in that area.

Spice Girls Limited v Aprilia World Service *[2002] EMLR 27*

The facts were:

A pop group was offered a contract with the manufacturer Aprilla to promote their scooters through advertising. All five existing members of the group took part in the filming of the commercial although all the group members knew that one very famous member of the group was about to leave. They failed to disclose this to Aprilla.

The dispute to be decided by the court was:

The court had to decide whether the band members failing to disclose that a member of the group was about leave the band amounted to a misrepresentation by conduct.

Use these questions to analyse the legal issues:

- What is the general rule in relation to silence?
- Are there any exceptions to this rule which is relevant in this case?

The principle of law applied/established was:

While silence does not usually amount to misrepresentation, a false statement of fact can be made without words but instead by the conduct of a party.

The outcome (the principle that applied to the facts) was:

A representation by being filmed and attendance at the photo shoot amounted to conduct which equated to a statement of fact that none of the band members was about to or intended to leave. This false statement of fact induced Aprilla to contract with the band.

20.3.2 Mistake

Shogun Finance v Hudson *[2004] 1 AC 919*

The facts were:

A "rogue" fraudster visited a Mitsubishi showroom and identified himself as D Patel. He completed the Hire Purchase forms to purchase a car and presented a stolen driving licence as proof of identify in the name of D Patel. The car dealer then sent the completed forms via fax to the claimant finance company who carried out the necessary credit checks in the name of the real D Patel before agreeing to provide finance for the purchase of the car. The rogue then paid a deposit (partly cash and partly cheque) and took the car away, which he then sold to the defendant Hudson. The finance company sued under the tort of conversion for damages.

The dispute to be decided by the court was:

The court had to decide whether the contract would be void for unilateral mistake as to identity and decide who should bear the loss between two innocent parties.

Use these questions to analyse the legal issues:

- What are the different rules relating to mistaken identity in the context of:
  - Face-to-face dealing;
  - Non–face-to-face dealing.
- Who was the rogue contracting with?
- Was this a case of face-to-face dealing or dealing at arm's length?

The principle of law applied/established was:

In cases of mistaken identity, a seller cannot pass on title if he does not have it (*nemo dat quod non habet*). Whether a contract of sale is void (and thus will not pass on title) depends on whether the unilateral mistake was about the identity (rather than the creditworthiness) of the buyer. In face to face transactions, the presumption is that it was not; in arm's-length transactions, the presumption is that identity was a term of the contract.

The outcome (the principle that applied to the facts) was:

It was decided that the contract was void for mistake as to identity as this was an arm's-length transaction as the contract between D Patel and the finance company (the rogue dealt face-to-face with the dealership, but the contract was with the finance company and this was done via fax). The company wanted to deal with the real D Patel, and as the real D Patel did not enter the contract, the contract was void for mistaken identity. Therefore Mr Hudson had to return the car.

20.3.3 Duress and undue influence

Royal Bank of Scotland Plc v Etridge (No.2) *[2001] UKHL 44*

The facts were:

This was a set of conjoined appeals. Conjoined appeals are where appeals arising out of a number of different claims are heard together by the appellate court because they all involve the same point of law. All of the claims in *Etridge* involved transactions where a wife used her legal interest in her family home as security for a loan to her husband. In all cases, the contract itself was between the wife and the lender; but the wife argued that the contract should be set aside because of undue influence by a third party, her husband.

The dispute to be decided by the court was:

When is a transaction between two parties affected by undue influence by a third party? And in cases involving loans, what steps must the lender take to avoid the contract being set aside?

Use these questions to analyse the legal issues:

- Should a bank only be put "on inquiry" where the borrower and the surety were married?
- Did this reflect modern society?
- What was the problem with the existing law requiring the surety simply to speak to a solicitor before the transaction?

The principle of law applied/established was:

Etridge included a number of important observations about the way in which undue influence could be proved. This included confirming that there was no requirement for "manifest disadvantage", that a presumption of undue influence could be established by showing a relationship of trust and confidence coupled with a transaction that "called for explanation", and doubt being cast on the "Class 1/2A/2B" terminology then in use.

However, the appeals considered in *Etridge* related more to when a lender would be put on inquiry, and what steps that then required the lender to take. The judgments in *Etridge* made it clear that a lender would be put on inquiry whenever one person stood as surety for a loan to another, and there was a non-commercial relationship between these people. Detailed guidance was then provided as to exactly what steps a bank would need to take. In particular, it was not enough for the surety simply to speak to a solicitor. The advice needed to be properly independent, given without the borrower present, and detailed enough to fully explain the risks of the transaction.

The outcome (the principle applied to the facts) was:

Because there were eight separate appeals, all based on the law prior to *Etridge*, various outcomes were reached.

Notes:

Lord Bingham noted in his judgment the wider societal importance of the case. He noted that if lenders were overly concerned that lending money based on using a family home as security might lead to the contract being set aside, they would become very reluctant to give such loans. He noted that many small businesses would and did rely on these kind of loans to raise funds.

20.3.4 Illegality

Nordenfelt v Maxim Nordenfelt Guns & Ammunition Co Ltd *[1894] AC 535*

The facts were:

The defendant was an inventor of weapons, running his own arms manufacturing company. On the sale of the company to the claimant, the defendant agreed to a clause restricting him from engaging in the trade or business of manufacturing guns for 25 years. The clause operated worldwide.

The dispute to be decided by the court was:

Could such a broad restriction of the defendant's trade be upheld?

Use these questions to analyse the legal issues:

- Is the law generally in favour of clauses in restraint of trade?
- When might such a clause be reasonable?
- Did the nature of the defendant's business change what would be reasonable?

The principle of law applied/established was:

The House of Lords held that, despite previous authority to the contrary, contract law would no longer distinguish between "general" and "partial" restraints on a person's trade. All clauses in restraint of trade would be treated the same, in that they were on the face of it void but would be upheld if they could be shown to be reasonable as between the parties and in the public interest.

The outcome (the principle applied to the facts) was:

It was therefore irrelevant that this clause was a "general" restraint (preventing the defendant from engaging in his trade anywhere in the world) rather than a "partial" restraint. The only question was whether, on these particular facts, the clause was reasonable. Given that the development and sale of weapons was an international trade, carried on with governments and leaders, in this instance it was reasonable for the clause to restrict the defendant from manufacturing or selling guns worldwide.

Notes:

Lord Herschell made the point in his judgment that business practices change with time and technology. He noted that older cases were based on a world where people could only travel or communicate quickly over short distances, but that today (in 1894) communication over hundreds of miles was almost instantaneous and goods could be delivered within a few hours. This shows how contract law must constantly adapt to changes in how business is done and contracts are made – and that this was as much an issue in 1894 as it is today.

20.4 Discharge of contract

20.4.1 Discharge by frustration

Davis Contractors Ltd v Fareham UDC *[1956] AC 696*

The facts were:

A building firm contracted to build council houses for a local council for a set price. The work was intended to take 8 months. However, the work took much longer than anticipated and agreed between the parties because there was a shortage in labour and materials which meant that the work took 22 months to complete. Because of this, the builders argued that the contract was frustrated.

The dispute to be decided by the court was:

Did the fact that the contract would now take much longer to perform and was now very costly for the building firm frustrate the contract?

Use these questions to analyse the legal issues:

- Was the contract impossible to perform?
- What is meant by the term "radically different"?
- Was performance in practice radically different from what had been expected?

The principle of law applied/established was:

A contract would only be frustrated if "without default of either party, a contractual obligation has become incapable of being performed because the circumstances in which performance is called for would render it a thing radically different from that which was undertaken by the contract".[1]

The outcome (the principle that applied to the facts) was:

The contract was not frustrated as it was not radically different from what the parties had intended from the outset. Just because a contract becomes more onerous, difficult, or expensive to perform, it is unlikely that a contract will be frustrated.

20.4.2 Discharge of contract

Cutter v Powell *[1795] 6 Term Reports 320*

The facts were:

Mr Cutter was contracted to serve on a ship sailing from Jamaica to Liverpool but died before he completed the journey. The captain of the ship refused to pay any of Mr Cutter's wages to his widow because he had failed to sail the whole voyage.

The dispute to be decided by the court was:

Was the widow claiming on behalf of the deceased estate entitled to any money given that Mr Cutter had not completely performed his contractual obligations?

1 Lord Radcliffe in *Davis Contractors Ltd v Fareham UDC* [1956] AC 696.

Use this question to analyse the legal issues:

- What is the entire performance rule?

The principle of law applied/established was:

Performance must be complete. In other words, it must be "precise and exact".

The outcome (the principle that applied to the facts) was:

The rule that performance must be "precise and exact" was applied. The deceased's action failed as Cutter had not completed his contractual obligations, and therefore the widow was not entitled to any proportion of Cutter's wages.

Notes:

Cases such as this one demonstrated how harsh the entire performance rule can be. As a result, a number of exceptions and qualifications have developed, as outlined in Chapter 15.

20.5 Remedies

20.5.1 Damages

Ruxley Electronics v Forsyth *[1996] AC 344*

The facts were:

The claimant agreed to build a swimming pool in the defendant's garden. The defendant sought to withhold payment for the work on the basis that the pool was not as deep as had been contracted for. The contract stated the maximum depth of the pool should be 7 feet 6 inches, but the pool as constructed had a maximum depth of 6 feet 9 inches. The trial judge made findings of fact that:

1. To reconstruct the pool would cost over £20,000, which was more than the initial price of the work, because the pool would need to be demolished and a new pool built; and
2. The shallower depth of the pool did not in any way decrease the value of the pool (or the value of the property as a whole).

The dispute to be decided by the court was:

What was the correct measure of damages for the claimant?

Use these questions to analyse the legal issues:

- How much would the claimant receive if awarded damages based on the cost of cure?
- How much would the claimant receive if awarded damages based on the difference in value?
- What would you do if you were the judge in this case?

The principle of law applied/established was:

Damages in contract law represent expectation loss. They are not punitive (intended to punish the defendant). In most cases, expectation loss will be calculated by reference to the cost of cure or the difference in value; but in exceptional circumstances where damages under either measure would be unreasonable or inadequate, damages can instead be awarded on a "loss of amenity" basis.

The outcome (the principle applied to the facts) was:

It was unreasonable to award the full cost of cure, because this was so high. The defendant would be creating a loss by insisting on demolishing and rebuilding the pool for no practical purpose; or the defendant would not carry out the work and would be unjustly enriched.

It was also not appropriate to calculate damages based on the diminution of value, because the defendant had suffered a loss – he had not got what he had bargained for.

Therefore, the only just measure of damages was a "loss of amenity" award.

Notes:

Across their judgments, the Law Lords made particular reference to ideas of common sense and doing justice between the parties. Arguably, the result was a compromise rather than a clear expression of legal principle – Mr Forsyth was awarded £2,500, just less than 10% of the total cost of rebuilding the pool. This was reflected in the fact that the type of damage award, loss of amenity, is a type of loss (loss of enjoyment) that is not normally recognised in most contract claims. The decision is an example of modern contract law preferring flexibility over the certainty offered by strictly applying inflexible traditional rules.

Cavendish Square Holding v Makdessi; ParkingEye v Beavis *[2015] UKSC 67*

The facts were:

> This case was the result of two conjoined cases: one in relation to commercial contracts (*Cavendish Square*) and one in relation to consumer contracts (*ParkingEye*). Both disputes related to liquidated damages clauses that were alleged to be unenforceable "penalty" clauses.

In *Cavendish Square* the claimants had entered into an agreement to buy the defendant's business. In breach of the agreement, the defendant had set up rival companies. The claimants argued that because the defendant was in breach of his fiduciary obligations, two clauses took effect under which the defendant (1) forfeited a large sum of money otherwise due as part of the purchase price, and (2) was required to sell his remaining shares to the claimants at a lower price.

In *ParkingEye* the defendant parked in the claimant's car park. The car park had a two-hour parking limit, but the defendant overstayed for an extra hour. The claimant demanded the £85 charge advertised in the car park as being due if a driver overstayed.

The dispute to be decided by the court was:

> What was the correct test to determine whether a clause would be unenforceable as a penalty clause? Were the clauses in the commercial agreement in *Cavendish Square* and/or in the consumer agreement in *ParkingEye* enforceable?

Use these questions to analyse the legal issues:

- Why was the existing test of whether the clause represented a "genuine pre-estimate of loss" in question?
- Why might parties include a liquidated damages clause in a contract?

The principle of law applied/established was:

> The penalty rule itself should not be abolished or extended, but the test for whether a clause was unenforceable as a penalty was. A clause requiring payment of a set sum on breach will be upheld if the party seeking to rely on the clause can show that they had a legitimate interest in ensuring performance and that the sum payable was not extravagant or unconscionable.

The outcome (the principle applied to the facts) was:

The clauses in *Cavendish Square* did not fall foul of the penalty rule. The claimants had a legitimate interest in protecting the goodwill of the business they had purchased for a very high sum of money and the amount involved (i.e. deduction from the sale price otherwise to be paid) was not extravagant or unconscionable. It was also relevant that the contract had been negotiated extensively with expert legal advice on both sides.

The clause in *ParkingEye* was also enforceable. The car park operator had a legitimate interest in efficient use of the car park, freeing up spaces for future users. The fine was similar to that charged in other local car parks and was not extravagant or unconscionable.

Notes:

Some of the Supreme Court Justices expressed concerns about the underlying foundations of the rule against penalties, suggesting this may be an area that requires further consideration in future.

20.5.2 Causation, remoteness, and the duty to mitigate

Hadley v Baxendale *(1854) 9 Ex 341*

The facts were:

The claimants ran a steam-operated mill for grinding corn. Part of the mill, the crank shaft, broke and the claimants arranged to send the broken part to a company which would manufacture a replacement. The replacement had to be exactly the same, so the old broken shaft had to first be delivered to the company making the replacement. The claimants contracted with the defendants for the defendants to deliver the broken shaft. Under the contract the delivery was agreed to be within two days of collection, but the defendants actually took seven days to deliver the broken shaft. Due to the delay, the claimants mill was unable to operate for a week longer than expected.

The dispute to be decided by the court was:

Could the claimants recover their lost profits during the delayed crank shaft repair from the defendants, or were the losses too remote?

Use these questions to analyse the legal issues:

- What is normal and abnormal loss?
- Could the defendants have expected the delay to cause these losses to the claimants?

- When the defendants were asked to carry a broken part, would they have known how quickly the part was delivered would affect the claimant's ongoing business?

The principle of law applied/established was:

It was held that damages for breach of contract would not be too remote where the loss being claimed either

1. Arose naturally according to the usual course of things; or
2. Was due to special circumstances which were known to both parties at the time the contract was made.

The outcome (the principle applied to the facts) was:

It was as likely that the claimants had already fitted a spare crank shaft, and were getting rid of the broken shaft than that the claimants were transporting the broken shaft in order to help make a replacement. So the loss did not flow naturally from the breach of contract, and so the first limb (normal) of the test was not engaged. No special circumstances were made known to the defendants (i.e. they were not told the mill could not operate until the shaft was taken away and used to make a replacement), so the second limb (abnormal) of the test was not engaged.

Notes:

While there have been many attempts to restate or reword the "two-limbed" test established in *Hadley v Baxendale*, it remains the key test for remoteness of damages in contract law.

20.5.3 Specific performance and injunctions

Co-operative Insurance Society Ltd v Argyll Stores (Holdings) Ltd *[1998] AC 1*

The facts were:

The claimants were landlords of a shopping centre. They granted the defendants a lease to operate a supermarket at the shopping centre. The supermarket was the largest and most popular shop so was considered a major reason why other companies operated shops at the shopping centre. Fifteen years into the 35-year lease, the defendants closed the supermarket in breach of their lease which imposed a positive covenant (a promise to do something) to keep the store open and trading.

The dispute to be decided by the court was:

It was agreed that the defendants were in breach of contract. The defendants were willing to pay damages as a result. But could the claimants instead obtain an order for specific performance?

Use these questions to analyse the legal issues:

- What would be the potential problem with an order to carry on the business for the next 20 years?
- What exactly does "carrying on a business" mean in the context of a supermarket?

The principle of law applied/established was:

Specific performance is a discretionary remedy. It has not traditionally been granted to make a defendant carry on a business. There were a number of good reasons for that approach:

1. The court will not grant specific performance where constant supervision is required (i.e. the parties could return again and again to court arguing about whether the contract was being complied with)
2. The court will not grant specific performance where the order itself cannot be precisely drawn up (i.e. what is required is vague or ambiguous)
3. Requiring a defendant to carry on a business might unjustly enrich the claimant, because the defendant has to operate at a great loss to comply. The claimant could then demand the defendant paid a much higher sum than would have been due in damages, to escape from the contract.

The outcome (the principle applied to the facts) was:

There were a number of good reasons which, taken together, justified the principle that the court would not award specific performance to require the carrying on of a business. As such, the order would not be granted.

Notes:

In fact, the defendant was able to assign (give to another company) the lease prior to the House of Lords hearing the appeal, so the injunction would never have actually taken effect if it had been granted. The case still needed to be decided because it would decide who would have to pay the (substantial) legal costs of the dispute.

20.5.4 Unjust enrichment

Attorney General v Blake *[2000] 1 AC 268*

The facts were:

The case concerned a spy who was a member of MI6. Due to the confidentiality of his work, he signed a declaration under the Official Secrets Act 1989 not to disclose information associated with his work, including after his employment terminated. After being imprisoned for 10 years he escaped and fled to Russia. He then published an autobiography which contained secrets; this was in breach of the Official Secrets Act 1989 and amounted to a breach of his employment contract not to disclose certain information associated with his work. He was paid in total £150,000.

The dispute to be decided by the court was:

Whether the Attorney General could prevent Blake from claiming the remaining amount due to him for the publication of the autobiography. In addition, the courts had to consider whether restitution could be used in this case to stop Blake from benefitting or being unjustly enriched from the crimes Blake committed and the breach of contract.

Use these questions to analyse the legal issues:

- What is meant by restitution?
- What is the purpose of this remedy?
- Why is this remedy exceptional and not usually awarded?

The principle of law applied/established was:

In exceptional cases the courts may order a defendant to account for profits in breach of contract.

The outcome (the principle that applied to the facts) was:

Blake was ordered to account for profits made by the publication of the autobiography. The House of Lords considered Blake's case as exceptional.

21 Answers to multiple choice questions

21.1 Chapter overview

This chapter provides the answers to the multiple choice questions at the end of each chapter of the book.

DOI: 10.4324/9781032642161-27

21.2 Chapter 1 – offer and acceptance

Question 1

Answer

Option A is correct. In auctions, each bid constitutes an offer and acceptance takes place on the fall of the hammer. As this has not taken place in response to Syreeta's bid, there is no contract with Syreeta. Therefore, B and E are incorrect, as there is no contract with Syreeta.

However, there seems to be a contract with Leyla using the objective approach to determine whether there was a valid acceptance. Even if subjectively Leyla wasn't sure she wanted to bid, an objective observer would see her raising her hand as an indication she was bidding (making an offer). C is incorrect as there is a potential contract with Leyla, and D is incorrect as the courts look at the objective approach and not the subjective approach in determining whether a valid contract has been formed.

Question 2

Answer

Option D is correct. The offer is a unilateral offer. Coffee R Us are bound by it, but the people who read the advertisement are not. They do not have to turn up at 10 am or buy the coffee if they do not wish to. Therefore A is incorrect. B and E are also incorrect because there is no need to communicate a promise in advance to accept a unilateral offer – acceptance is via performance. The unilateral contract has been accepted, therefore C is incorrect.

Question 3

Answer

Option B is correct. The general rule in relation to advertisements is that an advert is an invitation to treat (therefore A and E are incorrect). There has been a valid offer by Uche, met with a counteroffer by Hamid. The contract has been formed when it would be reasonable to expect Hamid to listen to his answering machine, which is on 4 July (because it is available to be heard during his business hours), and thus D is incorrect. The onus will be on Hamid to check the answering machine; therefore C is incorrect.

21.3 Chapter 2 – intention to create legal relations, certainty, and capacity

Question 1

Answer

Option E is correct. This is a domestic agreement made in a domestic context over a family dinner; therefore, A and B are incorrect. The rebuttable presumption in a social or domestic agreement is that there is no intention to create legal relations. However, this presumption can be rebutted by proving evidence to the contrary; therefore, C and D are incorrect. Therefore, A is incorrect because the agreement has been evidenced in writing and the court will give effect to such promises if there is enough evidence to rebut the presumption.

Question 2

Answer

Option C is correct. The ITablet is not classified as necessaries, and therefore the contract is voidable. Therefore, Eden has the discretion to cancel the contract. A is therefore incorrect, as the ITablet is not classified as necessaries. B is incorrect, as Eden does have the discretion to cancel the contract and the contract is voidable. D is incorrect, as the contract is voidable and not void. E is incorrect, as it does matter whether goods are necessaries.

21.4 Chapter 3 – consideration

Question 1

Answer

Option C is correct. The general rule in relation to part payment of a debt is that it does not discharge the full debt. In other words, it is not a good consideration. Therefore, A and B are incorrect, as the theatre can demand the full amount. Promissory estoppel cannot be used as a sword (i.e. as grounds to make a claim), and therefore D is incorrect. E is incorrect in terms of providing consideration. Simon has provided sufficient consideration for the initial agreement, but no consideration at all for the promise to accept a lesser sum.

Question 2

Answer

Option A is correct. This question focuses on an existing contractual duty. As Elise is already under an existing contractual and is only doing what she is contractually obliged to do, it will not amount to fresh consideration unless Elise is going over and beyond her existing contractual duty. Here Elise has gone over and beyond her existing contractual duty and provided fresh consideration by agreeing to deliver an extra 80 leaflets; therefore, B is incorrect. The promise has not been given after the act, and therefore it is not past consideration; therefore, C and E are incorrect. There is consideration; therefore, D is incorrect.

Question 3

Answer

Option C is correct. Generally, past consideration is not good consideration, and therefore unless any exceptions apply it will not be good consideration. Therefore, A is incorrect. No exceptions apply here; therefore, D is incorrect. This question does not relate to executory and executed consideration; therefore, B and E are incorrect.

21.5 Chapter 4 – privity of contract and rights of third parties

Question 1

Answer

Option B is correct. At common law, the rule of privity does operate to prevent a third party from enforcing a contract they are not party to. However, an exception to the rule is created by the Contracts (Rights of Third Parties) Act 1999 which allows a third party, who is identified in the contract, to enforce a term either because it expressly provides that they may, or because the term is for their benefit and on a "proper construction" of the contract it appears the parties intended the term to be enforceable by the third party. Here, the wife is expressly identified in the contract, the terms stating she will receive a massage and access to the sauna complex are for her benefit and there is no evidence to rebut the presumption that the parties did not intend the term to be enforceable.

A is not correct. There is no evidence that the contract expressly states the wife may enforce it.

C is not correct. The husband has not personally suffered any loss, as he was not due to receive the treatments.

D is not correct. The contract can be enforced under the 1999 Act. There is no relevant collateral contract here, nor would such a contract affect whether the spa contract could be enforced.

E is not correct. The rule of privity is subject to the 1999 Act where it applies.

Question 2

Answer

Option C is correct. The contract cannot be enforced by the daughter in her own name. The rule of privity prevents a third party from enforcing a contract. The contract was made when the daughter had no title to the home and so was not for her benefit. The Contracts (Rights of Third Parties) Act 1999 does not apply, and therefore A is incorrect. There is no relationship of agency, and therefore B is incorrect. This is not a contract with the sole purpose of enjoyment, pleasure or entertainment, and in any event this allows the party to the contract to claim for a third party's loss, not for a third party to claim directly. E is thus incorrect.

However, because the daughter is the executor of the homeowner's estate, she is able to bring an action in the name of the homeowner. This would allow her to seek the remedy of specific performance, which would have the effect of ordering the gardener to complete the work. As such, C is correct and D is incorrect.

21.6 Chapter 5 – express terms and incorporation of terms

Question 1

Answer

Option E is correct. Where one party makes it clear that such importance is attached to a statement that they would not contract were the statement not true, it is likely that statement will be a term of the contract. In this instance the pet food company had no interest in contracting for hay that was not pesticide-free, so this was a fundamental part of the contract.

A is incorrect because there is no requirement for independent verification, although had the farmer suggested the company did verify for themselves this may have made the statement less likely to be a term.

B is incorrect because the statement was not mere sales talk; it was a crucial fact of great importance to the other party.

C is incorrect, because the relevant specialist knowledge in this case would be that of the farmer, who had grown the hay.

D is incorrect because the delay is, in any event, quite short; and more fundamentally it is highly unlikely to outweigh the importance of the statement.

Question 2

Answer

Option D is correct. An exclusion clause can be incorporated by signature, but also by reasonable notice or by a consistent course of dealing (and thus E is incorrect). In order to incorporate a clause via reasonable notice, the degree of notice must be reasonable, but notice must also come before or at the time of contracting. Because the clause was not notified to the visitor until after she made her contract (by buying her ticket at the park entrance) notice has come too late. The degree of notice is therefore irrelevant and thus B and C are incorrect.

One visit to a theme park in two years is not a consistent course of dealing, and so A is also incorrect.

Question 3

Answer

Option E is correct. The vehicle being roadworthy is a wide term which could be breached in many different ways. It could be breached in a very minor way, such as one of the windows being dirty (as for a car to be legally roadworthy, the windows must be clear); or in a very serious way, such as having no engine. As such, the court is unlikely to classify the term as either a condition or a warranty (making answers A, B, and C incorrect).

If the term is innominate, the remedy will depend on the consequences of breach. Here, the consequences are very minor – paying £125 to refill the brake fluid – and the florist still has substantially the benefit of the contract (a working van). As such, while damages in the sum of £125 would be payable for the breach, the florist cannot terminate the contract (and so answer D is incorrect).

21.7 Chapter 6 – implied terms

Question 1

Answer

Option C is correct. While the customer does intend to use the car for some purposes connected to her work (commuting), she is still purchasing the car as a consumer under the meaning of the Consumer Rights Act 2015, and so this Act applies. As such, answers B, D, and E are not correct.

The issue with the car is not that it is not of satisfactory quality as a car in itself – it is that it is not fit for a particular purpose which the buyer made known to the seller at the time of contracting. Therefore, the correct answer is C rather than A.

Question 2

Answer

Option C is correct. The court has used the business efficacy test to imply the term. The term has not been implied because of legislation, so A is incorrect. Nor has it been implied because of existing trade practice or custom, so D and E are incorrect. The term is implied into this particular contract, rather than all contracts of this type, so it has been implied in fact rather than in law. Therefore B is incorrect.

21.8 Chapter 7 – the interpretation of terms

Question 1

Answer

Option D is correct. The court will not be overly literal or rely on dictionary definitions (thus A is not correct). It will use the natural and ordinary meaning of the words, which in this instance is very likely to refer to the overall weight being carried by the vehicle rather than whether a person happens to be sitting in the passenger seat. Therefore C describes the right approach but the wrong outcome. The subjective understanding of the parties, and their pre-contractual negotiations, are not relevant factors considered by the court, thus B and E are also incorrect.

21.9 Chapter 8 – exemption clauses and unfair contract terms

Question 1

Answer

Option B is correct. The contract is between the university acting for purposes relating its business, while the students are acting for purposes outside their trade, business, craft, or profession. As such, the university is a trader and the students are consumers and fall under the Consumer Rights Act 2015. This means the Unfair Contract Terms Act 1977 does not apply and answers C and D are incorrect.

Under the 2015 Act, any term purporting to exclude liability for personal injury or death as a result of negligence is automatically unfair. This will include Clause 34. Clause 49 will be subject to the test of unfairness – it will not take effect if, contrary to the requirement of good faith, it causes a significant imbalance in the parties' rights and obligations under the contract to the detriment of the consumer. Answer A is incorrect because it suggests Clause 49 will be automatically considered unfair.

Answer E is incorrect. Signature is a valid means of incorporating terms into a contract.

Question 2

Answer

Option E is correct. This is an agreement made between two companies in the course of business. Therefore the relevant legislation is the Unfair Contract Terms Act 1977, not the Consumer Rights Act 2015. As such, the fairness test does not apply and so answers B and D are incorrect.

Under the 1977 Act, clauses relating to contractual liability are subject to the reasonableness test (not automatically void, making answer A incorrect). Given that this is a contract between two large companies, it is likely that there is not inequality of bargaining power. Both parties have access to legal advice and are commercially experienced. It is therefore unlikely that the court would consider a negotiated clause such as this to be unreasonable – so answer E is correct and answer C is not correct.

21.10 Chapter 9 – misrepresentation

Question 1

Answer

Option E is correct. The statement made by Leroy is more than just sales talk – it is clearly a statement that is likely to help persuade a buyer to choose to enter into a contract to purchase the car. Therefore it is not a mere puff, and answer D is incorrect. The statement is likely to be considered negligent, as given the obvious issues, it will be hard for Leroy to show he believed the statement to be true and that he had grounds for that belief. Thus answers B and C are incorrect. Rescission is usually available for negligent misrepresentation (unless any bars apply), so A is incorrect.

Question 2

Answer

Option E is correct. In order to determine the correct test for reliance upon the statement, the type of misrepresentation needs to be determined. The seller has no expertise and is relying on the word of an expert, so on the facts given it is likely that she believed the statement to be true and had reasonable grounds for that belief. Therefore answers A and D are incorrect.

For innocent (and negligent) misrepresentations, the claimant must show that but for the statement they would not have entered into the contract. The "actively present to his mind" test only applies to fraudulent misrepresentations. Therefore answer B is incorrect. Applying the law to the facts, the buyer has purchased the clock to use as decoration on film sets and in photoshoots. Whether the clock actually keeps accurate time is not relevant for these uses, so it is unlikely that but for the statement the sale would not have taken place, and so answer C is incorrect.

21.11 Chapter 10 – mistake

Question 1

Answer

Option D is correct. The circumstances mean that the presumption in relation to face to face transactions apply, i.e. that you intend to deal with the person in front of you. There is no evidence Hamish took specific steps to ensure he was only dealing with "Sirianna", and so his mistake is about the creditworthiness of the person in front of him (Aisha). Therefore A and C are incorrect.

Because the original contract is not void for mistake, good title to the ring passes to Aisha and on to Oscar. Therefore Oscar can keep the ring as he has acquired good title (making E incorrect). This also means B is incorrect, because while there has been a misrepresentation, this does not prevent the title passing under the contract of sale – it just means that if Oscar can find Aisha, he has a right against her for damages. Rescission would not be available (i.e. returning the ring) because it would affect Oscar's legal right to the ring, and rescission cannot be granted where it would affect a third party's rights.

21.12 Chapter 11 – duress and undue influence

Question 1

Answer

Option E is correct. There is a clear threat to destroy or damage property belonging to the barber. The threat has caused the barber to enter into the revised contract.

Answer A is incorrect because a threat by a party's agent or employee can constitute a valid form of illegitimate pressure.

Answer B is incorrect because there is no requirement for the threatened party to protest at the time the contract is made (although such a protest may be evidence of causation).

Answer C is incorrect because the clear threat makes this a case of duress rather than undue influence.

Answer D is incorrect because the threat is to cause criminal damage, an unlawful act.

Question 2

Answer

Option A is correct. A lender is put on inquiry where one person agrees to stand surety for another, in a transaction which is to the surety's disadvantage, and there is a non-commercial relationship between them. The transaction is to the younger sister's disadvantage because she stands to lose her flat and does not seem to benefit from the loan, as the money goes to her elder sister's business. The bank has failed to then discharge this notice by not ensuring the younger sister met with an independent advisor without her older sister present.

B is incorrect because there is no evidence that the bank knew of the undue influence – the notice was constructive, not actual.

C is incorrect because there is no evidence of undue influence on the part of the bank itself.

D is incorrect because all that is required is a non-commercial relationship, not a relationship of marriage.

E is incorrect because the advice given was insufficient. It should be given by an independent advisor and should have been given without the other party present.

21.13 Chapter 12 – illegality

Question 1

Answer

Option A is correct. All restraint of trade clauses are on their face void (and therefore answers D and E are incorrect). To rely on such a clause, a party must show that it was reasonable both between the parties and in the public interest. Restricting an employee from using the basic skills developed during their employment is unreasonable, so answers B and C are incorrect. However, a six-month restriction on approaching existing customers of his former employer may be considered a reasonable restraint.

21.14 Chapter 13 – discharge by frustration

Question 1

Answer

Option B is correct. Where a sufficient part of the contract can still be performed, the contract will not be frustrated; therefore, A is incorrect. The overall purpose (a luxury weekend break) still exists. If a contract is frustrated, parties are discharged from any future obligations under the contract; therefore, C is incorrect. There is no such thing as partial frustration. D is incorrect, as parties cannot choose to affirm the contract if the contract is frustrated. E is incorrect, as the contract cannot be discharged because full performance has not taken place. As will be explained in the next chapter, Chapter 14, anything less than full performance will be a form of breach, and there will be a claim in breach of contract for a sum of damages for Tanika and Tyrone.

Question 2

Answer

Option A is correct. Impossibility renders a contract frustrated, as impossibility will mean that the contract is radically different from what the parties had in contemplation at the time of forming the contract. Therefore, B is incorrect as the contract is radically different and therefore likely to be frustrated, and therefore C and E are also incorrect. D is incorrect as performance has been made impossible.

21.15 Chapter 14 – discharge by agreement, breach, or expiry of time or other specified event

Question 1

Answer

Option B is correct. Anticipatory breach occurs when one party informs the other of their intention not to perform before the due date. As this is the case on the set of facts there will be a breach, meaning C is incorrect. Carlos will be able to elect to discharge the contract and claim damages from 24 March, therefore A is incorrect. The breach goes to the root of the contract and therefore the breach is not a warranty and the remedies available for breach of warranty are not damages and termination; therefore, D is incorrect. For the reasons mentioned above on the set of facts, there appears to be an anticipatory breach, and therefore E is incorrect.

21.16 Chapter 15 – discharge by performance

Question 1

Answer

Option A is correct. Performance must be "precise and exact" any deviation means that performance is not "precise and exact". There are exceptions that apply: Bathroom R Us will argue that they have substantially performed, therefore B and E (bearing in mind choice) are incorrect, but not complete completion, therefore C is incorrect. D is incorrect, as the defects are not irrelevant.

21.17 Chapter 16 – damages

Question 1

Answer

Option D is correct. While the usual measure of damages is expectation loss, based on the position the parties would be in had the contract been performed as expected, it will not be possible for the court to predict how many copies the prospective book would sell, therefore making the losses speculative. Therefore answers A, B, and C are incorrect.

Instead, the court will award reliance loss damages based on the amount expended by the ghostwriter in reliance on the contract. This will be the cost of six months of travel and research work. There is no mention of a liquidated damages (an amount agreed between the parties) clause in the contract, so answer E is incorrect.

Question 2

Answer

Option B is correct. The usual measure of damages is expectation loss. In a sale of goods case, this will usually be calculated using the difference in value. The cyclist expected to receive £14,000 in exchange for her bike. She has received £13,500 instead, so she has £500 less than expected.

A is incorrect because the cyclist has lost out in comparison to the position she would have been in had the original contract been performed as intended.

C and D are incorrect because the £1,000 difference between the true value of the bike and the price paid is irrelevant. The cyclist only ever expected to receive £14,000, not £15,000.

E is incorrect because this is the full value of the bike, and the cyclist has received £13,500 already in exchange for the bike.

Question 3

Answer

Option B is correct. The court has the discretion in each case to determine whether a clause requiring a set sum to be paid on breach will be upheld (and so answers C and D are incorrect). The club has a legitimate interest to protect (having a new stadium ready for the start of the football season) and the amount of the clause is not extravagant or arbitrary – it is the amount the club will lose because of the need to pay to use an alternative stadium. As such, the clause will be upheld and answer E is incorrect. Answer A is incorrect because the claim is for liquidated damages, not unliquidated damages to be set by the court.

21.18 Chapter 17 – causation, remoteness, and the duty to mitigate

Question 1

Answer

Option E is correct. In order for a loss not to be too remote, it must be in the reasonable contemplation of both parties. This can be because it is a loss arising naturally in the usual course of things; or because it is a result of special circumstances known to both parties. In this situation, the special circumstances were known to both parties at the time the contract was made, so it was in their reasonable contemplation and will not be too remote.

Answers A and B are incorrect because if the loss falls under the "second limb" of special circumstances known to the parties, it does not need to be shown to be a loss in the usual course of things or for which the defendant assumed responsibility.

Answer C is incorrect because this is the reason the loss can be recovered, not the reason why it cannot.

Answer D is incorrect because this is not a loss arising in the usual course of things. It is out of the ordinary and so falls under the second limb rather than the first limb of the test.

21.19 Chapter 18 – specific performance and injunctions

Question

Answer

Option D is correct. Specific performance will not be granted in a contract for personal services, because the court would be compelling someone to do something against their will, breaching their rights to liberty.

Answers A and B are incorrect because they do not take account of this crucial principle.

Answer C is incorrect because the painting is unique – so it is unlikely that damages would be a sufficient remedy. Answer E is incorrect because there is no "clean hands" issue here – this refers to where a party has behaved unconscionably or immorally in relation to the contractual dispute.

21.20 Chapter 19 – basic principles of restitution and unjust enrichment in the context of termination of contract

Question 1

Answer

Option D is correct. Eze has a strong claim for the £5,000, as this is the extra amount he has had to pay (compared to what he would have paid David) to obtain what he contracted for, a new kitchen. David is in breach of contract, so there is a claim, therefore answer C is incorrect. Answers A and B are incorrect because it is highly unlikely there is an claim for account of profits here. The contract is in a commercial context, there is no sensitive context for the obligation (e.g. it is not a matter of national security or similar), and the relationship between the parties is not fiduciary. What David has done may be morally unpleasant, but it does not justify the law giving Eze money he has not himself lost. Answer E is incorrect because specific performance is not available in contracts for personal services (see Chapter 18).

Index

Note: Page numbers in *italic* indicate a figure and page numbers in **bold** indicate a table on the corresponding page.